Forever Welcomed

Forever Welcomed

A Study on God's Impartial Love for All

OGHOSA IYAMU

MOODY PUBLISHERS
CHICAGO

© 2025 by
OGHOSA IYAMU

All rights reserved. No part of this book may be reproduced in any form without permission in writing from the publisher, except in the case of brief quotations embodied in critical articles or reviews.

All Scripture quotations, unless otherwise indicated, are taken from the Holy Bible, New International Version®, NIV®. Copyright © 1973, 1978, 1984, 2011 by Biblica, Inc.™ Used by permission of Zondervan. All rights reserved worldwide. www.zondervan.com The "NIV" and "New International Version" are trademarks registered in the United States Patent and Trademark Office by Biblica, Inc.™

Scripture quotations marked (ESV) are taken from The ESV® Bible (The Holy Bible, English Standard Version®), copyright © 2001 by Crossway, a publishing ministry of Good News Publishers. Used by permission. All rights reserved.

Scripture quotations are from the ESV® Bible (The Holy Bible, English Standard Version®), © 2001 by Crossway, a publishing ministry of Good News Publishers. ESV Text Edition: 2025. The ESV text may not be quoted in any publication made available to the public by a Creative Commons license. The ESV may not be translated in whole or in part into any other language. Used by permission. All rights reserved.

Scripture quotations marked (NKJV) have been taken from the New King James Version®. Copyright © 1982 by Thomas Nelson. Used by permission. All rights reserved.

All emphasis in Scripture has been added.

Content in Day One of Week Three is based on a post the author wrote that originally appeared on the She Reads Truth website: https://shereadstruth.com/the–lord–provides–in–the–wilderness–2/

Edited by Whitney K. Pipkin
Interior design: Puckett Smartt
Cover design: Kaylee Lockenour Dunn
Cover artwork: "Rambling Pastels" by Erin Hanson. All rights reserved.
Cover texture of linen © 2025 by goldnetz/Adobe Stock (109145724). All rights reserved.
Author Photo: Savvy Rose Photography

Library of Congress Cataloging-in-Publication Data

Names: Iyamu, Oghosa author
Title: Forever welcomed : a study on God's impartial love for all / Oghosa Iyamu.
Description: Chicago : Moody Publishers, [2025] | Includes bibliographical references. | Summary: "This six-week Bible study traces the tapestry of God's impartial love through the Bible-a love grounded His character, not our abilities or status. In a world darkened by social, economic, cultural, racial, and political partiality, this is an invitation to reflect God's heart for life in His eternal kingdom"-- Provided by publisher.
Identifiers: LCCN 2025012068 (print) | LCCN 2025012069 (ebook) | ISBN 9780802437174 paperback | ISBN 9780802468635 ebook
Subjects: LCSH: God--Love--Biblical teaching | Bible--Study and teaching | BISAC: RELIGION / Biblical Studies / General | RELIGION / Christian Living / Personal Growth
Classification: LCC BS544 .I93 2025 (print) | LCC BS544 (ebook) | DDC 231--dc23/eng/20250609
LC record available at https://lccn.loc.gov/2025012068
LC ebook record available at https://lccn.loc.gov/2025012069

Originally delivered by fleets of horse–drawn wagons, the affordable paperbacks from D. L. Moody's publishing house resourced the church and served everyday people. Now, after more than 125 years of publishing and ministry, Moody Publishers' mission remains the same—even if our delivery systems have changed a bit. For more information on other books (and resources) created from a biblical perspective, go to www.moodypublishers.com or write to:

Moody Publishers
820 N. LaSalle Boulevard
Chicago, IL 60610

1 3 5 7 9 10 8 6 4 2

Printed in Colombia

This book is dedicated to those who have ever felt unwelcomed, struggled to receive God's love, or made the mistake of loving others with partiality.

There is hope.

CONTENTS

The Impartial Love of God	8
Week One: Impartial Creator	12
Week Two: Impartial Covenant	38
Week Three: Impartial Communion	70
Week Four: Impartial Call	98
Week Five: Impartial Christ	132
Week Six: Impartial Church	166
Background Materials	203
Acknowledgments	209
Notes	211
About the Author	217

The Impartial Love of God

When a pastor invited me to teach on James 2 for a women's Bible study, I hadn't spent much time immersed in its words.

I opened its pages anticipating the usual from James—practical wisdom, a challenge to live out faith in real life, encouragement not to see suffering as an obstacle, and so forth. But what I didn't see coming was a direct onfrontation and *revelation* that those women and I desperately needed.

What we didn't expect was that a message written to a first-century church could feel so distinctively timely, as if it were written directly to us.

The second chapter of James describes God's often overlooked attribute of impartiality. God's radical and generous hospitality welcomes the undeserving, regardless of their past, position, or power. God's impartiality goes far beyond what God simply does; it's who He is and how He loves. It is carved into His character and displayed in His ways.

And this truth is not isolated to the book of James.

God's impartiality is a central theme running throughout the entire biblical story, pointing us to His glory.

What began as a teaching in the book of James has overflowed into the pages you are now reading, because I wholeheartedly believe that you too are invited to know and love—even to grapple with—the God who reveals His impartiality and calls us to the same.

Welcome.

Forever Welcomed invites us to lift our eyes and hope as we trace one of God's often overlooked attributes through the grand story of Scripture.

This study offers a cultural and historical lens, reflective questions, and intentional response sections for each day. It guides us individually and collectively, as the people of God, to receive and reflect God's impartial love.

More than just a study, this book is a call to both impartial love and merciful action, an invitation to receive and reflect God's vision for life in His kingdom where all who come are forever welcomed.

In this six-week study, we will discover a powerful antidote to the divisions that often separate us from God and from one another. We will see how we can respond to God's open invitation—His eternal welcome—and be radically transformed so that we too can extend that same love to others.

> *"Truly I understand that God shows no partiality, but in every nation, anyone who fears him and does what is right is acceptable to him."*
>
> (ACTS 10:34-35 ESV)

READ, RECEIVE, RESPOND

At times during this study, we'll look through the lens of an ancient Israelite. It's important to note that many of the passages we'll explore weren't typically read but were passed down orally from one generation to the next (Deut. 6:4–7). In Jewish culture, studying Scripture was about both hearing and *living* in accordance.[1] It involved engaging with the text in a way that shaped not just the way someone thought but the *way they lived*.

The Hebrew word *shema*, meaning "to hear" (Deut. 6:4), captures this practice of active listening and responding to God's Word. *Shema* requires full attention with your whole heart, which leads to obedience. The biblical story describes the practice of *shema* as listening so thoroughly that the truth permeates every part of your life, shaping your decisions, relationships, actions, and even words.[2]

In Hebrew thought, *shema* is closely linked to the word "remember." And that's intentional. As mentioned earlier, true listening isn't just about hearing and moving on. It's about recalling God's Word in a way that compels a response, even something as simple and powerful as gratitude. It's the idea that hearing and doing are two sides of the same coin. You remember in order to act.

Our approach in this study is designed to guide you through this ancient practice, helping you engage with Scripture in a way that invites deep listening, intentional remembrance, and faithful obedience. To that end, each week we will:

Read—seeking to comprehend the content and context of the text.

Receive—acknowledging who God is and inviting His truth to transform us.

Respond—accepting the call of action and walking in obedience.

As we *shema*—read, receive, and respond—my hope is that we will increasingly embody God's words.

This study is divided into daily sections. You will also find some Tugging the Threads boxes exploring some of the Hebrew background shaping the rich tapestry of Scripture. But there's no pressure to complete a day's work in one sitting. In fact, I might encourage you not to. Pause when you need to, return back when you need to, and reflect as long as you need. The focus here isn't about ticking boxes or reaching a goal quickly—it's about savoring the sweetness of communion with God.

Remember, the Bible wasn't written in our cultural moment. Studying and understanding it takes prayer, time, and effort.

> *It's the hymn since the beginning of creation,*
> *We see resounding through the ages.*
> *Crafted with wisdom and poetry on eternal pages.*
> *It's the rhythmic drumbeat of the prophets' plea,*
> *We hear reverberating through the decades,*
> *It's the anthem of God's kingdom, we feel ringing out loudly*
> *A forever welcome.*
> *This is God's decree: to love without partiality.*

> – OGHOSA IYAMU

WEEK ONE | IMPARTIAL CREATOR

Impartial Creator

This week, we will trace God's impartial love demonstrated through His role as Creator. From the beginning, God imprints His image and bestows equal worth upon both male and female. Through this act God reveals His character and establishes the pattern of human dignity throughout Scripture.

From the start, God welcomed humanity . . .

This is life in the ancient Near East: Families rise in their stone homes, greeted by the melodic chanting of voices as the light of dawn breaks over the horizon.

Grand temples and large buildings line the cities' sand-dusted streets, featuring carved images of different gods and political leaders, each of them objects of worship.[1]

The air is dense, mingled with burning incense. The Babylonian, Mesopotamian, and Egyptian creation stories were expressed through everyday life experiences.

Being an Israelite then required moving through a world filled with various conflicting stories about how the world began. The creation narratives of neighboring cultures were the lenses through which many saw and understood their identity, their purpose for existence, and their relationship with the divine.

As we slowly zoom into the Bible's creation story, we will see how God stands apart from the other stories bombarding the ancient Israelites. God's impartial love shapes our understanding of who we are and, more importantly, who God is.

WEEK ONE | DAY ONE

Made in God's Image

Before you begin, ask God to open your eyes to His impartial love, that you may read it, receive it, and respond faithfully.

READ:

Genesis 1:26–28, Deuteronomy 33:2

RECEIVE:

In your own words, how would you briefly describe the cultural setting during the time the book of Genesis was delivered to Moses? *(Use information provided in the opening section to help.)*

According to Deuteronomy 33:2, how did Moses receive the revelation of the creation story?

Refer to the Background Materials on page 203. Who was Moses, and what role did he play in Israel's history and in writing parts of the Bible?

Don't miss this. **Moses was raised in the wisdom and influence of Egyptian royal culture. Yet through God's inspiration, he wrote the first five books of the Bible (Deut. 31:24–26). Considering Moses' background, what makes him uniquely positioned to proclaim the true and better story that sets itself apart from the creation myths of surrounding cultures?**

The very first line in Genesis 1:1 introduces God by the name of *Elohim*,[2] which means "God the Creator." This name reflects God's unmatched power, authority, and sovereign will in bringing the world into existence.

Read Genesis 1:26–27 and fill in the blank:
Then God said, _____, in our likeness. . . . So God created man in his own image, _____ he created them.
In your opinion, what is one way these verses portray God's impartial love?

WEEK ONE: IMPARTIAL CREATOR

TUGGING THE THREADS: The word "image" in Hebrew, *tselem* (צֶלֶם) describes an object that has been carved out and shaped with intention. It's rooted in the idea of "to shade," as in a shadow of something else. Many kings had images created to be a distinct resemblance to their appearance.[3]

God uses *tselem* when He speaks of creating humanity as living, breathing bearers of His image. Unlike the lifeless statues of Egyptian gods,[4] which were merely carved representations, God created us to truly reflect His nature. We are meant to mirror His love, justice, mercy, and presence in the world.

When Moses and the Israelites heard the word *tselem* in the context of God's creation of man, they likely couldn't help but think of the idols and false gods of Egypt, those empty statues that filled the temples and lined the streets.

According to Genesis, what does God's image represent to humanity? Circle the best answer.

   a) An empty and powerless symbol

   b) A living reflection of His character that we are called to emulate

   c) A God who is nothing like us and whose character attributes we cannot emulate

Imagine being an Israelite, hearing that you were created to be a "carved-out" reflection of God's very image, a shadow of His love, patience, kindness, and justice. So much so that when others look at you, they will see not just a human being but a reflection of God's character.

How might that truth change the way you see yourself, your purpose, and your identity? How would it transform the way you interact with others, knowing that every action, every word, could be a testimony to the God whose image you bear?

RESPOND:

Romans 1:25 says, "They exchanged the truth about God for a lie, and worshiped and served created things rather than the Creator—who is forever praised. Amen."

This verse warns against people worshiping created things rather than the Creator. When we look at our culture today, we can see the same kind of thing happening.

Where do you see the truth about God's character and nature being exchanged for a lie? What influences in your daily life (media, relationships, or cultural norms) tempt you to diminish reflecting God's image?

As we end our day reflecting on being made in God's image, how can you resist these pressures and encourage others to do the same?

WEEK ONE | DAY TWO

Included in God's Plan

Before you begin, ask God to open your eyes to His impartial love, that you may read it, receive it, and respond faithfully.

READ:
Genesis 2:16–22, Genesis 1:27–28

In the ancient Near East, social status and power weren't determined by gender alone. Instead, a person's standing in society depended on factors such as wealth, whether they were a slave or free, family heritage, and more.[5] In our modern, Western world, it's easy to interpret Genesis through a gender-based lens, thinking of it in terms of a rigid male-female superiority system.

But that's not how the Israelites would have heard this story. Their society was different from ours because gender roles did not dominate the conversations. Their world operated as a more intricate social web of status where occupation, gender, and age assigned positions and power.

And when we take a breath and pause to truly reconsider the assumptions we bring—those that simplify and flatten the rich texture of a world where power wasn't dictated only by gender—the reality is that the world the Israelites knew was different. It was more intricate, more layered, and more shaped by the dynamic interplay of social structures than we often imagine.[6]

FOREVER WELCOMED

What makes Genesis 2 so uniquely countercultural is that it offers a vision of humanity that differs from (and in some ways contrasts with) the stories that surrounded the Israelites. In many ancient Near Eastern narratives, women were missing entirely or portrayed as mere servants of the gods.[7]

In the patriarchal world of ancient Greece, women were seen as inferior, sometimes even thought of as "broken men" or dangerous.[8] In wealthier households, women were secluded in the inner quarters of the home, hidden away from guests, seldom seen in public, and kept out of the social sphere.[9]

Again, the Bible offers a radically different plan for humanity: Both men and women are made in the image of the living God (Gen. 1:27). *Together*, every woman and every man are crowned with the same dignity by God. This is a status of unparalleled worth.

And in that truth, we find an invitation to receive and extend the impartial love of God.

RECEIVE:
Look up Genesis 1:27–28. What command is given and to whom is it directed?

The Command	Directed To

Did Adam and Eve do anything to earn God's impartial love or dignity?

Read Ephesians 1:4. How does this contrast with the way the world sets conditions and boundaries around who is considered "worthy" of dignity and inclusion?

Read Genesis 2:18 and look up the meaning of "helper" (*'ēzer kenegdo*) in the Background Materials on page 204. In your own words, what does it mean?

How does understanding Eve as a necessary ally[10]—created to partner with man—confirm, slightly shift, or completely change the way you read Genesis?

Fill in the blanks of the following psalms where the word *'ēzer kenegdo* is translated in various ways *(I used the NIV here, but feel free to use your preferred translation):*

Psalm 121:1–2 "I lift up my eyes to the mountains—_____
_____? _____ comes from the LORD, _____
_____."

Exodus 18:4 "The other was named Eliezer, for he said, '_____
_____; he saved me from the sword of Pharaoh.'"

Psalm 115:9–11 "All you Israelites, trust in the LORD —
_____ and shield. House of Aaron, trust in
the LORD —_____. You who fear him,
trust the LORD—he is _____."

20   FOREVER WELCOMED

Circle True or False. If false, write the correct answer.

True or False: The term "helper" (*'ēzer kenegdo*) used in the context of Eve implies a lesser role (Gen. 2:18).

True or False: The term *'ēzer*, translated as "helper," is often used in the Bible to describe God as the ultimate supporter, showing us the significant role in strength and partnership.

True or False: The term *'ēzer* in the Bible often means active help on behalf of someone, especially in military situations, as seen in Psalm 121:1–2.

In Greek culture, where gender was used as one form of status, how does the fact that God intentionally created both genders with equal dignity challenge that cultural mindset that viewed women as less valuable?

Do you sometimes struggle to see your own value or feel truly included in God's plan? Underline any of the following reasons that might sometimes hold you back . . .

shame from my past	feelings of unworthiness
doubts about my abilities	comparison to others
fear of failure	wavering trust in God's promises

WEEK ONE: IMPARTIAL CREATOR

TUGGING THE THREADS: There's a hope-filled word in Scripture called *ebenezer* that connects to the word *'ēzer* we just studied. It comes from two Hebrew words: *eben* (אֶבֶן) and *'ēzer* (עֵזֶר). *Eben* means "stone" or "rock,"[11] and *'ēzer* means help, signifying God's active, tangible support, especially in times of crisis.[12]

Together, these words form Ebenezer—literally "Stone of Help"—serving as a powerful picture of God's unwavering faithfulness and His role as our constant source of rescue.

In 1 Samuel 7:12, Samuel sets up a stone and calls it Ebenezer, saying, "Thus far the LORD has helped us." More than a marker for memory, this rock stood as a testimony, a living memorial that God is the ultimate source of our support, the unshakable Rock in the midst of every battle. Just as the Israelites leaned on God's help to face their physical and spiritual struggles, we too are called to depend on His strength to overcome.[13]

RESPOND:

How can you set up reminders, like an Ebenezer, to mark His faithfulness in your life? In what areas of your life can you pause and say, "Thus far, the LORD has helped me"?

WEEK ONE | DAY THREE

Independent of Culture

Before you begin, ask God to open your eyes to His impartial love, that you may read it, receive it, and respond faithfully.

READ:

Genesis 3:1–13

RECEIVE:

In ancient Near East culture, the serpent had a rather interesting symbolism with meanings that changed depending on the cultural contexts. Egyptian culture revered the serpent as an important symbol that represented supreme power and divine rule. One example is the Egyptian uraeus used as a decorative headdress for pharaohs, which mimicked a cobra (snake-like). It was seen as representing life and protection from threats.[14]

However, in the lands of Mesopotamia, the serpent took on a much darker form. It was often associated with chaos and destructive forces that threatened to undo the very order of creation, a sort of de-creation.[15] In Hebrew thought, the serpent in Genesis 3 takes on that same chaotic, disruptive role.

When we consider the cultural backdrop of the serpent, it adds layers of depth to our understanding of Genesis 3 and other passages in Scripture (Num. 21:4–9; Ex. 7:8–12; Rev. 12:3–9). Imagine hearing Genesis 3 as an Israelite, knowing the cultural significance of serpents in the surrounding world. The serpent's temptation wasn't just a subtle suggestion to disobey but a cosmic, defiant challenge to the very world order established by God.[16]

The call to God's people, then, is to resist the forces of disorder and destruction that seek to undo God's good creation. Instead of believing the competing narratives of the nations, God's people are to trust in the authority and goodness of the One who created and sustains all things.

Read Genesis 3:1–5. In Eve's response to the serpent, how does she change or add to God's command (Gen. 3:2–3)? Complete the fill-in-the-blank below by selecting words from the word bank.

Word Bank: **amplifies, diminishes, minimizes**

> She quotes God as saying: "You must not eat fruit from the tree that is in the middle of the garden."
>
> Eve _____ the directive by adding "and you must not touch it."

> She quotes God, saying: "We may eat fruit from the trees in the garden."
>
> Eve _____ the delight by saying "we may eat" rather than "you are free to eat" (Gen. 2:16).

> She quotes God as saying: "or you will die."
>
> Eve _____ the danger with "or you die" rather than "you will certainly die" (Gen. 2:17).

24   FOREVER WELCOMED

How do the subtle changes in Eve's response to the serpent reflect her growing shift in perspective? Is she starting to live independently from God's truth, or from the serpent's lies?

The enemy's goal is to make bondage look like freedom and freedom look like bondage.

In the ancient Near East, trees weren't just seen as physical objects; they were believed to be divine resources providing abundance, immortality, and the blessing of the gods.[17]

The Tree of Life in the garden of Eden was God's personal invitation to His people, a call to live in intimate trust and complete dependence on His wisdom (Gen. 2:9).

Read Proverbs 3:18 and fill in the blanks:

"She is a tree of life to those who take hold of her; _____ _____." In Proverbs, wisdom is described as a "_____" for those who embrace it.

Read Psalm 1:1–3. What are two distinctive characteristics of a tree planted by streams of water that would not be true of a dying tree? How does this imagery deepen your understanding of the vital need to stay rooted in God's Word for spiritual growth, strength, and endurance?

WEEK ONE: IMPARTIAL CREATOR

DESIRE + DECEPTION = DISOBEDIENCE

Read Genesis 3:6 again. *She saw.* It's always where it starts, isn't it? Eve's eyes saw the fruit, and she thought it looked good: good to the eye, good for food, good on the outside. But it was something God had forbidden. The original sin of humanity was to judge by what one could see, not by what God had said.

I want to draw your attention to something before we move to our response time. The word *ta'awah* means "intensely desired," "appetite," and sometimes "lust."[18] In Genesis 3 we see this word *ta'awah* in action when Eve's desire was stirred by what she saw, leading her to disobey God.[19]

Matthew 6:22 says, "The eye is the lamp of the body." James 1:14 adds that "each person is tempted when they are dragged away by their own evil desire and enticed." For each of the following verses, read the passage and match it with what the subject saw. Then write what the subject did after seeing.

In Genesis 3:6, the woman saw . . .	Bathsheba
In 2 Samuel 11:2–4, David saw . . .	Sarai, Abram's wife
In Genesis 12:14–15, Pharaoh's officials saw . . .	The plunder
In Joshua 7:21–25, Achan saw . . .	The fruit

Read Matthew 6:22–23. What one word does Jesus use to describe the eye's relationship to the body? Why is it important to consider where we allow our gaze to wander and to linger?

RESPOND:

On Day 1, we witnessed God bestowing honor and dignity upon humanity at creation. One of the ways God does this is by giving us the freedom to choose—to make daily decisions. This is what we call *free will*. Though we often don't realize it, this freedom is a vital expression of the dignity God has granted to each one of us.[20]

Consider the main ways you take in information today. What visual temptations are currently drawing you away from God's commands and toward sin?

-

-

Let's Respond with Prayer:

Father God, help me notice the deceiving temptations that exist both around me and inside me. Lord, I confess I have allowed my eyes and mind to wander aimlessly. I need Your help to guide my gaze.

Would You fill me with a hunger for Your Word and a desire to live in a way that honors You and others? Guard the minds of those I love [insert their names here]. Renew our spirits together, and help us find rest in the freedom that comes from following You fully. Thank You for Your grace and for always calling us back to You.

In Jesus' name, we pray. Amen.

WEEK ONE | DAY FOUR

Identity Reimagined

Before you begin, ask God to open your eyes to His impartial love, that you may read it, receive it, and respond faithfully.

READ:
Genesis 3:1–19

RECEIVE:
The Tree of Life in Eden was God's invitation to partake in the very good life He Himself offered, one of trust and dependence (Gen. 2:9). But eating from the forbidden Tree of the Knowledge of Good and Evil brought judgment, not life. That's because Adam and Eve stepped outside of what God had intended for them.

In Genesis 3:9, God asks Adam, "Where are you?" after Adam and Eve ate from the forbidden tree. What does this question reveal about God's welcome, even in times of failure or sin?

Highlight or circle below everything this passage indicates is true about His nature.

God desires intimacy with us, even after we have fallen into sin.

God wants honesty and accountability from us.

God's approach is gentle and relational; He doesn't lead with shame.

God's question reflects His all-knowing presence and power paired with grace.

God values relationships over mere condemnation, giving us space to confess and be restored.

Consider Genesis 3:9. How do you envision God when you fall short? Do you see Him as distant, keeping His love at arm's length? Or do you imagine Him pursuing you, welcoming you back with relentless grace?

If we're being vulnerable: How do you react when someone else's sins or weaknesses are exposed? Do you pull away in judgment or discomfort? Or do you draw near with grace and truth, offering the same compassion you would hope to receive?

Read Genesis 3:12–13 again, and pay close attention to Adam and Eve's responses. Can you think of a time you found yourself showing partiality to your own sin by shifting blame?

How does this kind of partiality toward personal sin contrast with God's impartial judgment of all sin (Gen. 3:16–19)?

How would seeing through God's impartial lens encourage the way you approach confession, repentance, and surrender today?

This gospel is for you too.

Read Genesis 3:14–20. Write down three ways you see God's mercy—His gracious welcome toward humanity even in the midst of His judgment.

1.

2.

3.

Genesis 3:15 is a thread of hope right after Adam and Eve tasted the bitter fruit of disobedience. In the aftermath of their sin, God gave His first redemption promise known as the protoevangelium, the first announcement of good news.

This promise reaches beyond Eden across all of history as it sets the stage for God's great plan to redeem humanity.

God's justice may confront our sins, but His mercy makes a way for us to return again and again.

Even in their shame, He comes.
Even in their hiding, He seeks.

On Day Two, we learned that the term "helper" given to the woman also describes God's help. How do you think the promise in Genesis 3:15 points to the woman's role in redemption?

Read Galatians 4:4–5 and fill in the blank.

> But when the set time had fully come, God sent his Son, _____, born under law, to redeem those under law, that we might receive adoption to sonship.

Though Eve was the first to be tempted and to succumb to sin, Scripture shows that God, in His grace, offers the woman (and the man) a *reimagined identity*. In Genesis 3:15, when it seems like everything has fallen apart, God promises *help*— a future redemption through the woman's "seed."

And though Eve would face pain, hardship, and suffering as a consequence, God's promise indicates that her lineage would result in ultimate victory over evil. The weight of her failure would not be the final word spoken over her life (Gen. 3:20). God is in the business of reimagining identities.

Read Luke 4:18–19. How does the promise in Genesis 3:15, referring to the "seed," look forward to Christ and His mission on earth to bring a new identity to humanity?

JESUS OUR JUBILEE

In the Old Testament we see how God established a yearly cycle, a pattern meant to bring justice and equity to the people of Israel. During every seventh year a Sabbatical year occurred. The Jubilee year occurred on the fiftieth year after seven cycles of seven years had passed (Lev. 25:1–7).[21]

The Jubilee year was a special period during which people were offered a chance to start anew; land was returned to its rightful owners and debts were wiped away, freeing those who had sold themselves into servitude. During this year of new beginnings things that had gone wrong could be made right.

As we fast-forward to the New Testament, in Luke 4:18–19, Jesus picks up this promise as He reads from the book of Isaiah: "The Spirit of the Lord is on me . . . to proclaim the year of the Lord's favor." With these words, Jesus is announcing the arrival of the ultimate Jubilee. Jesus is saying, "I am the fulfillment of everything the Jubilee represented."[22] He offers the deep, soul-satisfying liberation that only God can bring: freedom from spiritual debt and bondage to sin. He is our reset, our opportunity to begin again. In Jesus, the long-awaited Jubilee is no longer a year on a calendar, it's a reality unfolding in the lives of those who follow Him.

He is our year of the Lord's favor, and He welcomes us to be made new.

RESPOND:
How does today's study remind you that, no matter how far you've wandered or how broken you feel, God is ready to welcome you back to Himself?

Jesus doesn't leave us where we are. But He also doesn't meet us in our brokenness and then walk away. He brings freedom to those who are captive. Sometimes, that freedom looks like Him opening our eyes to the truth that we are loved, pursued, and welcomed into His presence.

He welcomes you to give you an *identity reimagined.*

WEEK ONE | DAY FIVE

Impartial Love

Before you begin, ask God to open your eyes to His impartial love, that you may read it, receive it, and respond faithfully.

READ:
Exodus 33:17–23, Exodus 34:6–8

RECEIVE:
If God were to overlook sin, His love would cease to remain impartial, and His justice would no longer be righteous. This truth can be difficult for many to accept, but if we lean in, we'll see that this is not the antithesis of hope—it is the very source of it.

Scripture declares, "Righteousness and justice are the foundation of your throne; steadfast love and faithfulness go before you" (Ps. 89:14).

True impartiality means that God holds every soul to the same standard of holiness, regardless of past, position, or power. As Romans 2:11 clearly states, "For God shows no partiality." His love is not swayed by the things that sway us. God's vision is never clouded by unrighteous bias or human frailty.

God sees us as we truly are without the distorted lenses of our self-made identities or the world's fleeting labels, but through the purity of His perfect gaze. And in that gaze, we see both the call to holiness and the invitation to restoration—offered freely, impartially, to all who would come.

And I wonder, could it be that His impartiality is what makes His love so outrageously glorious?

God's impartial love has two outcomes. For those who reject Him, it leads to eternal separation from God (Rom. 1:18). But for those who humble themselves before Him, it leads to restoration (John 3:17). *The same God who judges sin is the God who rescues sinners.* God's impartial love confronts sin, but it also welcomes us through redemption in Jesus Christ.

His impartiality is not a wall keeping us from His love; it's the very bridge that draws us back to Him again and again when we fall short (Rev. 19:11). It's wide enough and strong enough to cover all who accept His invitation. And what a glorious, yet scandalous, invitation it is.

In Exodus 33, Moses asks to see God's glory. Look up the word "glory" (*kavod*) in the Background Materials on page 204 and summarize its meaning in one or two sentences.

In response to Moses' request, God reveals His character to Moses (Ex. 33:19–20). What specific attributes of God's character does He proclaim to Moses in Exodus 34:6?

WEEK ONE: IMPARTIAL CREATOR

Moses said, "Show me your glory."

God responded, "I will show you my attributes, for in them, you will not only behold but experience my glory" (paraphrased).

Today, you and I don't need anything monumental to happen to experience the very glory of God. His glory isn't always found in grand displays or earth-shattering events. Often, it's in the seemingly ordinary moments of everyday life. Right now, as you read through this study about God's attribute of impartial love, you have the opportunity to encounter His character, and therefore His glory, right where you are.

His goodness, His mercy, His faithfulness—His impartial love, they're unfolding in the pages before you, inviting you to see Him, to know Him.

Exodus 34:6–8 reveals a God who is "abounding in love" but also "does not leave the guilty unpunished" (Ex. 34:7). There's a tension here, isn't there? One that cues you and me to pause, because we want to understand how love and justice can coexist perfectly within the nature of God. Allow yourself a second to sit in this tension.

Think briefly, where have you seen God's love and justice working in tandem this week?

Maybe it's in the way He's shown you grace when you thought you had exhausted it or how He's led you through moments of reckoning, by loving you enough to help you face the truth. How have the threads of love and justice knitted together helped you better understand the character of God?

If you're anything like me, there are times you hesitate to show impartial love—a love that isn't persuaded by personal preferences or past hurts. Maybe you're afraid that others will take advantage of your kindness or that if you let go of resentment, justice will not be served.

How does knowing that God's love is always tied to His justice help you breathe a little deeper and love a little freer?

RESPOND:

Where are you struggling to love impartially, without conditions or self-protection? Is there someone in your life God is asking you to love with open hands, trusting Him to handle the outcome? How would it change your heart to love not from a place of fear, but from a place of faith?

Forever welcomed—that's what we are. As we move through this study, my hope is that we experience the profound depth of God's impartial love. It's a love that actively reaches for us, invites us, and welcomes us every day, even now.

WEEK TWO | IMPARTIAL COVENANT

Impartial Covenant

This week, we will trace God's impartial love through His covenants. We'll follow each thread as it connects the covenants God made with His people: the promises of mercy in the midst of judgment through the covenant with Noah; the promise given to Abraham that set the stage for a blessing to all people; the law delivered through Moses; the kingdom established with David, and finally, the most intimate new covenant, now stitched on the hearts of all who follow Christ.

Secure in His Promises

Covenants in the ancient Near East were shaped by social structures along with political and religious life. These factors affected the way people operated daily and built trust and relationships with one another. However, much of life for these individuals was driven by the fear of fickle gods whose anger was unpredictable and whose favor was fleeting. People lived in constant anxiety, always striving to avoid offending these capricious deities, never truly knowing if they were safe or secure.

But the God of the Bible is different.

He offers His people safety and security through a covenant with clear, defined expectations. This is something the gods of other nations never provided. What sets the God of Scripture apart is not only His impartial nature but His willingness to bind Himself to sinners. Unlike the distant, changeable gods of the nations, the Lord invites His people into a relationship of trust and faith.[1]

Every covenant we read this week (Noah, Abraham, David, and the new covenant) reveals God's generous hospitality. He welcomes undeserving sinners not because of their merit but because of His merciful grace. These covenant promises are like well-worn trails, guiding us through the history (His-story) of God's redemption.

WEEK TWO | DAY ONE

Made in God's Image

Before you begin, ask God to open your eyes to His impartial love, that you may read it, receive it, and respond faithfully.

READ:

Genesis 9:1 (ESV), Matthew 28:19

RECEIVE:

Keep your eyes peeled. As we trace the storyline of Scripture, we discover a God who continually draws nearer—closer and closer—until He moves from simply dwelling with His people to dwelling *within* them.

When you hear the word "covenant," what emotions or thoughts stir within you? I feel . . .

☐ comforted ☐ hesitant ☐ doubtful

☐ curious ☐ betrayed

Have past experiences such as moments of broken trust, unanswered prayers, or unexpected pain made it hard for you now or in the past to fully trust God's covenant promises? Take a moment to ask God to help you see the beauty of His promises in the Bible.

In Genesis 9:1, what does God command them to do? Fill in the blank:

And God blessed Noah and his sons and said to them, "_____

_____."

What similarities do you see between God's repeated command to Noah and Jesus' command to His disciples (Matt. 28:19)?

Considering these two verses above, do you think God's commands to be fruitful are limited to the physical act of bearing children? Are there other ways they invite us to multiply God's character and image in the world? How might this broader understanding of multiplication shape the way we live out our calling today?

Childbearing in biblical times went beyond family building; it was deeply tied to one's sense of identity, security, and social standing. For many living in ancient societies, children were viewed as a direct sign of God's favor and blessing. On the other hand, barrenness, particularly for women, was often seen as a source of shame and social stigma and even, for some, a sign of God's disfavor.[2]

A childless woman in that culture might have easily believed, "God's favor and blessing are not upon me." (As an unmarried woman with no children, I can't say I haven't had those same thoughts at times.) But, as we'll uncover in our study, culture's narrative is often not the story the Scriptures tell. In fact, as we keep reading, we'll see together that God's grand story welcomes and includes the unlikely in miraculous ways. But to see the fullness of that story, you've got to keep reading . . .

Use the Background Materials on pages 204–205 to look up the two types of covenants, then summarize what each one means in your own words:

Suzerain-Vassal Covenant:

Royal Grant Covenant:

Read Genesis 9:8–17. Based on these two types of covenants, which one do you think is represented in this passage? Why?

TUGGING THE THREADS: In Western culture, we often admire rainbows as daring displays of color across the sky; however, there's much more than meets the eye. Beneath their surface, the Bible reveals how rainbows point to a larger story of God's covenant promise.

The rainbow is more than a picturesque arc; it's a profound message of peace.

In ancient times, after a battle, warriors would hang their bow horizontally to signal the end of a conflict, saying, "I no longer need to aim at the enemy." In Genesis 9:13–16, God uses this imagery to declare that He has "hung up His bow." The rain, once a symbol of judgment and arrows aimed at the earth, has ceased; it's been hung up in the clouds for all to see.[3] The rainbow, then, is far more than a stunning display of color, but a visible covenantal promise of God's mercy to humanity. As God declares in Genesis 9:11, "never again will there be a flood to destroy the earth."

As we journey through the covenants this week, let's pause and reflect on God's consistent mission throughout time.

As you read through God's covenant promises referenced in the passages below, underline or circle repeated words and phrases in the verses.

> **To Noah:** *"God blessed them and said to them, 'Be fruitful and increase in number; fill the earth and subdue it. Rule over the fish in the sea and the birds in the sky and over every living creature that moves on the ground'"* (Gen. 1:28).

> **To Abraham:** *"I will make you very fruitful; I will make nations of you, and kings will come from you"* (Gen. 17:6).

> **To David:** *"When your days are over and you rest with your ancestors, I will raise up your offspring to succeed you, your own flesh and blood, and I will establish his kingdom. He is the one who will build a house for my Name, and I will establish the throne of his kingdom forever"* (2 Sam. 7:12–13).

> **To Israel:** *"I will look on you with favor and make you fruitful and increase your numbers, and I will keep my covenant with you"* (Lev. 26:9).

> **To Jesus' disciples:** *"Therefore go and make disciples of all nations, baptizing them in the name of the Father and of the Son and of the Holy Spirit"* (Matt. 28:19).

WEEK TWO: IMPARTIAL COVENANT

Have you spotted the patterns yet? What theme do you see included in God's promises? Circle all that apply.

- Rule

- Multiplication

- Abundance

- Fruitfulness, spiritual and physical

In ancient Near Eastern societies, ruling was directly connected to the idea of blessing. To bless went beyond wishing someone well. It was a transfer of authority, a passing on of power and favor.[4]

Take a moment to glance over the verses we just looked at. How many times do you see God using the word "I"? Whose actions are enabling and empowering the covenant promises?

When studying biblical covenants, it's always important to remember that they originated within a collective society rather than the individual-focused culture you and I are familiar with today.[5] As you skim through the list of covenants, take note of how God's promises extend beyond individual relationships, inviting faith communities into His story.

His covenantal faithfulness isn't confined to one individual but extends to whole communities. His call goes beyond "you" to "us." As we walk through these covenants together, we'll see God's invitation has always been to unite His people in a shared journey. His faithfulness doesn't just bless the "one" but spills over into a whole, holy community, shaping generations to come.

RESPOND:

In what ways (both expected and unexpected) is God calling you by the power of His Spirit to be fruitful in this season of life? How are you multiplying the work He has done in your life and in the lives of others?

Remember, God's fruitfulness is not always measured by visible success. How can you trust that even in seasons of sowing or being stretched, God is still nurturing your growth?

WEEK TWO | DAY TWO

Included in God's Plan

Before you begin, ask God to open your eyes to His impartial love, that you may read it, receive it, and respond faithfully.

READ:

Genesis 12:1–3, Genesis 15:1–6, Genesis 17:1–8

RECEIVE:

Noah's descendants multiply and grow in number, but they fall short of keeping God's command. But God has a plan. God forms a new covenant with Abraham, who has walked faithfully and righteously before Him (Gen. 15:6).

The ancient Near East defined betrothal as a legally binding agreement that signified mutual commitment before the final stage of "leaving and cleaving." Marriage required leaving behind the comfort and security of the father's household to create something new: a family built together. This physical relocation represented a change in loyalty, identity, and purpose.

As we'll see, the Bible uses the language and pattern of betrothal and marriage to describe God's relationship with His people (Hos. 2:19–20; Eph. 5:25–27; 2 Cor. 11:2). This metaphorical picture conveys God's intimate, covenantal relationship with His people.

Through this context, we will gain better clarity about Abraham's covenant call and the other covenants in Scripture that we'll study this week.

Read Genesis 12:1–3. What promises are included in the Abrahamic covenant? Fill in the blank. Place a star next to each *promise*.

I will make you into a great _____ (Gen. 12:2).

And I will bless _____; I will make _____ and you will be a blessing (Gen. 12:1–2).

I will bless _____ bless you, whoever curses you I will curse; and all peoples on earth _____ (Gen. 12:3).

What was Abraham's family background before God called him (Joshua 24:2)? Check one.

☐ A pagan—someone who worships multiple gods or idols.

☐ Monotheist—a worshiper of the one true God.

Did Abraham have to earn any status or merit before God chose him? How does this reflect God's impartial love?

In Genesis 12:1, God asks Abram to "go from your country, your people and your father's household to the land I will show you." How does this command reflect the customs of betrothal in the ancient Near East we learned earlier?

What three things did God ask Abraham to leave (Gen. 12:1)?

1.

2.

3.

Why do you think God asked Abraham to leave behind these three things? How does what Abraham was asked to leave relate to the blessing he was to receive? Check all that apply. *(Refer to the promises you starred earlier for guidance.)*

Security—to test Abraham's faith and willingness to trust God's leading beyond what felt secure.

Familiarity—to remove the familiarity that could keep him tied to the past.

Identity—to set him apart with a new identity for the special purpose of being included in God's plan.

Is there an area of your life where God might be asking you to let go of something—whether it's security, familiarity, or a false identity—in order to step into His greater plan for you? How can Abraham's example of trust and obedience encourage you to take that step of faith?

Read Genesis 15:1–7. After Abraham settles in Canaan, God appears to him in a vision to establish His covenant. Why do you think God chose to show Abraham this vision after and not before he left for Canaan?

The verse begins with the words, "I am the LORD" (v. 7). Ancient treaties often began with introductions of self-naming by the superior or king to assert their authority and set the terms of the agreement.[6]

Here, God does the same, declaring His authority and role in the covenant.

Then, God asks Abraham to do something that may seem strange to us today. He tells him to prepare a covenant ceremony. Abraham is to gather animals, cut them in half, and lay the pieces in two parallel rows.[7] Why this ritual? It was a common practice in ancient cultures to seal a serious agreement. In these ceremonies, the suzerain—or superior power—would walk between the severed pieces as a symbolic act of commitment. In this society, it would have been understood as if God were saying to Abraham, "If I do not keep My promise, may I become like these animals." The bloodied pieces served as a vivid reminder of the severe consequences if the covenant was broken (see Jer. 34:15–20).

Read Genesis 15:17–21. Describe or draw what passed between the separated pieces of animals in Genesis 15:17.

Who do you think it is that walks between the pieces of the sacrificial animals? And what led to your answer (Gen. 15:17)?

Maybe, like me, you read that, and you're almost convinced that this appearance is God Himself. Take a moment to consider other places in Scripture where God appeared as fire. The following are paraphrases of the passages where you will find the answers to fill in the blanks.

> **Exodus 3:2:** God appears to Moses in a _____ that is not consumed by the flames, revealing His holiness and calling Moses to deliver Israel from Egypt.

> **Exodus 13:21–22:** As the Israelites journey through the wilderness, God guides them by a _____ at night, symbolizing His presence and guidance.

> **Exodus 19:18:** When God descended on Mount Sinai to give the law to Moses, the mountain was covered in smoke because the Lord descended in _____, demonstrating His glory and power.

> **Acts 2:1–4:** On the day of Pentecost, those present saw what seemed to be _____ of_____ that separated and came to rest on each of them.

> **Hebrews 12:29:** Says that our God is a _____.

Read Genesis 15:17 again. Who didn't walk between the pieces of the sacrificial animals?

Can you even fathom this moment . . .
God Himself, walking between those pieces,
solemnly pledging to uphold His covenant with Abraham—
no matter what. What a love that the Creator of the universe
would swear by His own faithfulness. [8]

INCLUSION IN GOD'S PLAN

Now, who are Abraham's descendants? I can just hear the song, "Father Abraham had many sons" in my head. You too? God had promised Abraham that he would be the father of a great nation and that his family would inherit a great land (Gen. 12:2–3; 17:4–5). In return, Abraham and his descendants were to remain faithful to God (Gen. 18:19). As a sign of this covenant, every male in Abraham's household was required to be circumcised (Gen. 17:10–14), marking the Israelites as God's chosen people to be a light to the nations with the ultimate purpose of drawing all peoples near (Gen. 17:7–8).

Who are the "sons of Abraham" today? Fill in the blanks of these verses.

> Know then that it is those of faith who are _____.
> (Gal. 3:7 ESV)

> And if you are Christ's, then you are _____, heirs according to promise. (Gal. 3:29 ESV)

> That is why it depends on faith, in order that the promise may rest on grace and be guaranteed to all his offspring—not only to the adherent of the law but also to_____, who is the father of us all. (Rom. 4:16 ESV)

Look up Hebrews 11:6. What is required today to be included in God's plan?

We often focus on Abraham as the primary recipient of God's blessing, but when we look more closely, we see that God also extended His blessings to Sarah, a barren woman who was often despised in her culture, and to Hagar, a marginalized slave girl (Gen. 16:10; 17:15–16).

In a world where Sarah's infertility could have been perceived as a sign of God's judgment or disfavor, and Hagar's position as a slave meant she had no power or status, we might expect God to pass them by. But He didn't. His impartial plan included the unexpected too.

His love reaches even to the least likely among us: the forgotten, the overlooked, the marginalized, the undeserving. No one is beyond His reach.

RESPOND:

How does seeing God bless someone like Hagar—someone who's powerless, marginalized, and technically outside of the covenant—expand your understanding of God's love?

What does it tell us about the kind of people God chooses to welcome? Consider your own story.

WEEK TWO | DAY THREE

Independent of Culture

Before you begin, ask God to open your eyes to His impartial love, that you may read it, receive it, and respond faithfully.

READ:

Exodus 20:1–17

RECEIVE:

Have you ever felt . . . just kind of forgotten? Wondering if God will really come through on His promises? Maybe you're feeling it now.

This is where Abraham's descendants, the nation of Israel, found themselves at the beginning of Exodus—longing. God's people were enslaved in Egypt, crushed under the weight of oppression, waiting for a promise that seemed more distant memory than tangible hope.

They were desperate for God to show up and rescue them.

But lean in because this is right when God's rescue is put in motion. In Exodus 3, God appears to Moses and reveals His rescue plan to deliver. His people may have felt forgotten, but God makes it clear: He has seen their suffering; He has heard their cries, and He remembers the covenant He made with Abraham, Isaac, and Jacob (Ex. 3:7–8). God remembers His promise.

WEEK TWO: IMPARTIAL COVENANT

Yes, even when we forget, God does not. And even when we feel forgotten, God has not forgotten us.

God's rescue of Israel went beyond just physical freedom; God wanted to establish a covenant relationship with them, one that would redefine their identity. At Mount Sinai, God betroths Israel to Himself with covenant vows,[9] inviting them into a relationship marked by faithfulness, love, and obedience (Ex. 19:5–6; 20:1–3). The laws God gives are not arbitrary rules; they're reflections of His character to set and shape Israel apart as a kingdom of priests who would represent Him to the nations.

This is the story of God's people, the Israelites, yes. But in many ways, it's also the story of what God is doing in us.

Fill in the blanks for Ex. 20:1–2.

And God spoke all these words: "I am the Lord your God, _____ _____, out of the land _____."

Read Exodus 19:1–6. How do you see God's generous hospitality on display after they left Egypt?

What three titles does God promise His people if they obey the covenant? Fill in the blanks.

A _____ possession (Ex. 19:5)

A _____ of priests (Ex. 19:6)

A _____ nation (Ex. 19:6)

Based on Israel's response in Exodus 19:7–8 and what we've learned about covenants thus far in our study, what kind of covenant is being established here?

- A Suzerain-Vassal Covenant (a mutual agreement where the superior, the suzerain, sets the terms, outlining commands and offering blessings for obedience while also detailing consequences for disobedience from the subordinate, the vassal).[10]

- A Royal Grant Covenant (unconditional, where the superior makes promises to the subordinate without requiring a mutual return).[11]

Read Deuteronomy 7:7–8. Did the Israelites do anything, possess any special merit, or have any qualities that earned God's choice?

Have you noticed language similar to what we read earlier in Exodus also in the New Testament used to describe the church? Read 1 Peter 2:9, and then complete the following:

Chosen _____ (1 Peter 2:9)

Royal _____ (1 Peter 2:9)

A holy _____ (1 Peter 2:9)

Look again at Exodus 19:5-6 and 1 Peter 2:9. What pattern do you notice in the language used to describe God's people in the Old and New Testaments?

God consistently demonstrates a pattern of shaping an imperfect and flawed people for Himself—set apart and holy—*independent of culture.*

Take one more look at those titles—*chosen, royal, holy.* These are words that set His people apart. The world often parades costly, counterfeit versions of what God has already freely given to His people. The belonging it offers often comes in the form of titles we must earn and statuses we can lose. They can fade as quickly as they appear.

What God offers is infinitely better. Look up 1 Peter 1:4 and write what God offers us that's better.

God's people observed many festivals, one being the Feast of Weeks, called Pentecost. This Jewish celebration originally began to conclude the first fruits of the wheat harvest.[12]

It was on this very day of Pentecost that God delivered His commandments to Moses on Mount Sinai (Ex. 19–20). God's voice thundered across the shaky mountain that had been enveloped with fire and smoke as He inscribed His law into cold stone tablets.

But the day would come when those same laws would no longer be written on stone but etched into the souls of humanity.

And though His people's hearts would fail and their feet falter from the path of obedience, God's plan was not derailed (Ex. 31:18). He was not finished. When we turn to the New Testament, Pentecost takes on even greater significance as the day the Holy Spirit was poured out in tongues of fire on Jesus' followers (Acts 2).

Just as God once carved the Ten Commandments on stone tablets, now He inscribes His law in a new way—on the hearts of His people through the Holy Spirit, fulfilling the promise in Jeremiah 31:33: "I will put my law within them and write it on their hearts."[13]

Look up Acts 2:37 and fill in the blank. It says when the people heard the apostles' message, "They were _____."

Can you hear it? The gentle pricks of God's Word, no longer etched in cold stone—but now alive—cutting to the very heart of His people. This Word is alive and sharper than any two-edged sword (Heb. 4:12).

God's writing is active, ongoing, and happening right now, even as you read and study His Word. God is writing His laws on the hearts of His people. Through His Word and by His Spirit, He is transforming us, shaping us into the image of His Son.

RESPOND:

How would it change your outlook in circumstances or situations if you saw God's conviction as an invitation rather than forsakenness (Heb. 12:6)?

In what ways do you see God shaping and sharpening you, even (or perhaps especially) on your most difficult days?

WEEK TWO | DAY FOUR

Identity Reimagined

Before you begin, ask God to open your eyes to His impartial love, that you may read it, receive it, and respond faithfully.

READ:

1 Samuel 8

RECEIVE:

As we read in 1 Samuel 8, the Israelites make a bold and tragic demand: They want a king. They look around at the neighboring nations, seeing their influential kings and their royal power, and the Israelites crave that visible stability. Their request is not just for a ruler, though. It is a rejection of the reality that God Himself is their King, their Protector, their sovereign Defender. They want someone they can physically see, someone they can touch, someone who can lead them into physical battle, someone who will *be like* the kings of other nations.

When their first-chosen king falters, God sends the prophet Samuel to find another—one after his own heart. But God's criteria for the king will be much different from the people's.

Read 1 Samuel 16:10–13 and answer the following questions:

Who was David, and what was his occupation (1 Sam. 16:11)?

Where did David fall in the order of his siblings (1 Sam. 16:10–11)?

Read 1 Samuel 16:7. What does God remind Samuel, the faithful prophet and leader, not to judge by?

While humans tend to focus on what's visible—status, strength, or outward beauty—God looks at the heart, valuing inner character, intentions, and faith.

Look up the words "appearance" and "look" in the dictionary. Summarize in your own words what they mean.

Appearance:

Look:

What does 1 Samuel 16:7 reveal about God's impartiality? (See "Impartiality" in the Background Materials on page 206 for help.) How does God show us the contrast between human judgment and His own?

Why do you think it's important for us to see that even Samuel, a godly leader, was tempted to show partiality? What lesson or warning does this offer to everyone, including leaders?

WEEK TWO: IMPARTIAL COVENANT

In this culture, the youngest son was often regarded as the servant and inferior to the older,[14] both within the family and society. Inheritance and land were typically given to the firstborn in double portions, both within the family structure and society, leaving younger siblings with little inheritance.[15] This cultural hierarchy could place the youngest son at a lower status, with less influence and opportunity.

In 1 Samuel 16:12, David is described as physically handsome. But God's admonishment to the prophet tells us that Samuel was not looking at his physical appearance so much as his cultural qualifications for leadership. In the context of ancient Near Eastern culture, Samuel knew that kingship was typically reserved for the eldest, the strongest, and the most capable in men's eyes. Samuel, fully aware of these cultural norms, knew that choosing David and anointing him to be king would be . . . well, absurd.

But that's exactly what God does. Once again, God flips the script. God's kingdom is not based on influence, hierarchy, or external appearances; it's about the heart.

In 1 Samuel 16, we see God's surprising and sovereign choice to elevate the least likely candidate of the brothers. God sees what others overlook. And He is always in the business of reshaping identities.

God sees the heart, not social standing.

Can you recall a time when you were tempted to focus on outward appearance or worldly qualifications instead of seeking and trusting God's choice?

Have you ever found yourself drawn to the coworker or the child who's just easier to deal with? Or to the person who thinks like you, acts like you, or makes life a little easier? What would it look like to surrender that bias and impartially love like God does?

Read 2 Samuel 7:12–16. Here, God establishes a covenant with David, a promise that extends far beyond David's immediate descendants. In these verses, God makes three powerful promises to David. What are they?

Your _____ will endure forever (2 Sam. 7:16).

Your _____ will endure forever (2 Sam. 7:16).

Your _____ will endure forever (2 Sam. 7:16).

Read Acts 13:22–23. The apostle Paul speaks in the synagogue and says the promises made to David have been fulfilled through whom?

RESPOND:

Let's recall our earlier conversation. Consider someone—whether in your present or past—whom you've judged based on outward appearances or how similar they seemed to you. As you reflect, circle any of the following that resonate with you.

☐ I have looked down on someone because of their disability.

☐ I have preferred someone because of their socioeconomic status.

☐ I have thought more or less of someone because of their ethnicity.

☐ I have unfairly judged someone because of their gender.

☐ I have disregarded the intelligence of someone because of their age—younger or older.

☐ I have overlooked the skills of someone because of their education level.

☐ I have deemed someone not worthy because of their physical appearance.

☐ I have taken less interest in someone because of their job.

Rehearse the words of Psalm 145:8: "The LORD is gracious and compassionate, slow to anger and rich in love." Take a moment to sit quietly before the Lord and reflect. Ask God to reveal the next step of obedience He is calling you to take. Maybe it looks like . . .

Confession: Bringing hidden sins or struggles into the light before God and community.

Repentance: Turning away from sin and aligning your heart with the will of God found in His Word.

Reconciliation: Making a phone call to seek forgiveness or make peace in a relationship.

Surrender: Letting go of personal preferences and biases that are not from God.

Prayer: Committing to a deeper, more intimate communion with God.

Serving: Stewarding your gifts to bless and spend time with others who may not be like you.

"Come now, let us settle the matter," says the LORD.
"Though your sins are like scarlet, they shall be as white as snow;
though they are red as crimson, they shall be like wool."
(Isa. 1:18)

No matter how deep the stain of our sin, God's offer of forgiveness cleanses us completely. He longs to restore us and to give us a reimagined identity in Him. And this offer isn't just for someone else; it's for *you*.

WEEK TWO | DAY FIVE

Impartial Love

Before you begin, ask God to open your eyes to His impartial love, that you may read it, receive it, and respond faithfully.

READ:
Matthew 26:26–28, Luke 22:19–20, and John 6:53–56

RECEIVE:
First-century cultures demonstrated unity and loyalty through shared meals.

In the New Testament, the Last Supper is recorded in all four gospels, which adds another layer to this cultural practice of sharing a meal. Jesus is the generous Host, offering fellowship that is both personal and communal. He welcomes the undeserving who trust in Him to partake in His body and blood, uniting His people to Himself and one another through the actions He alone has taken. Through this act, we enter into a shared experience with Jesus and are bound together in a covenant of grace.

This moment inaugurates the new covenant. As Hebrews 10:20 (csb) explains, "He has inaugurated for us a new and living way through the curtain—that is, through His flesh."

Jesus' sacrifice opens the way for us to approach God. Through His broken body and shed blood, the door is now wide open (John 10:9). The Last Supper, then, is not simply a meal. It represents the consecrated doorway to true, eternal fellowship with God.

Fill in the blanks below.

Matthew 26:26–28: "This is _____, which is poured out for many for the forgiveness of sins." **Luke 22:19–20:** "This cup is _____, which is poured out for you." **John 6:53–56:** "Whoever eats my flesh and drinks my blood _____, and I in them."

If you and I were to peek into this first-century Jewish meal of Jesus' Last Supper, we'd likely witness it taking place on a mat, or low table with everyone reclining on cushions, as was the custom (Matt. 26:20). Around this table was a mix of misfits, tax collectors, fishermen, doubters, and even a betrayer. Some were steadfast in their devotion, while others wrestled with unbelief and wavering faith. This intimate gathering was a clear picture of God's welcome into His kingdom. The flawed, the wealthy, the poor, the haves, and the have-nots all are invited into the presence of the One who offers redemption.

In Matthew 26:26, as Jesus broke the bread, what memories would have flooded the minds of the Israelites? (See Ex. 12:14–20.)

Imagine being an Israelite, hearing Jesus' words after years of celebrating Passover. What other images from Matthew 26:26–29 likely filled their minds?

WEEK TWO: IMPARTIAL COVENANT

As one of these disciples you would have watched the breaking of the bread and pouring of new wine, and your mind would undoubtedly have drifted back to the Passover, the centuries-old celebration of when your ancestors the Israelites were delivered from slavery in Egypt. You would remember the lamb's blood on the doorposts, a sign of God's protection, and the meal set with symbolic foods like lamb, unleavened bread, and bitter herbs. All of these things prompting you to recall God's faithfulness then and here and now.

And if that weren't enough, you and the other disciples would have also mentally wandered back to the Feast of Unleavened Bread, which came right after Passover and represented purity by removing leaven (symbolizing sin) from the bread they ate.

And now, in this moment, how do you perceive Jesus reinterpreting it all right before their eyes? Fill in the blanks:

- He is showing them that He Himself is the true _____ (John 1:29), the ultimate _____ of Life (John 6:35)—the fulfillment of everything these ancient stories had pointed to.

- It's as if each of the festivals of Israel's history—the _____ (Ex. 12:11), the Exodus, the Feast of Unleavened _____ (Ex. 12:17)— were being woven together in this one meal with Jesus, who is the embodiment of God's salvation.

- It represents a powerful moment when everything they thought they knew about God's salvation was suddenly made visible.

It is in this setting that Jesus extends
an open invitation to the new covenant.

Circle True or False: The new covenant serves as the culmination, fulfillment, and perfection of the previous covenants made by God with His people. **Explain your answer.** (Hint: Think about how Christ's role in the new covenant offers assurance and hope in ways the earlier covenants could not.)[16]

Circle True or False: In the Last Supper, Jesus vividly symbolizes Himself as the living Passover, representing Israel's story of salvation. He is the once-for-all sacrifice for sin. Explain your answer.

Now, let's return briefly to that moment we talked about earlier—the setting of the Last Supper. Picture again who is gathered around that table: a betrayer, a tax collector, a fisherman, and others from different walks of life. How does this diverse group, every person with their own flaws and stories, portray God's impartial love?

God's welcome of people with diverse pasts and flaws completely flips our cultural understanding and challenges us to rethink who we deem worthy of an invitation to our tables. But remember, God's invitation extends far beyond the disciples at the table.

WEEK TWO: IMPARTIAL COVENANT

What is one way this gathering embodies the message and ministry the disciples were called to carry into a fractured and partial world? (See Matt. 28:19.)

Before we wrap up today, let's look closely at something Jesus shared with His disciples during this supper.

Read John 6:56. What do you think Jesus meant by "eating His flesh" and "drinking His blood"? Check all that apply:

☐ Jesus is using metaphorical language to describe the intimate, spiritual relationship between Himself and His followers.

☐ It represents identification with Christ.

☐ To "eat His flesh" and "drink His blood" is to fully abide in Him, as He says in John 15:4 (CSB): "Remain in me, and I in you." A radical expression of God's love, the depth of Jesus' sacrifice, and the means by which believers receive eternal life.

RESPOND:

Jesus gave a new command during the Last Supper within the context of a personal relationship.[17]

> A new command I give you: Love one another. As I have loved you, so you must love one another. By this everyone will know that you are my disciples, if you love one another. (John 13:34–35)

What do you think happens when we try to follow Jesus' commands and imitate Him without spending intentional time with Him (John 15:4)?

If your love was the only evidence, would the people you interact with know you are a disciple of Jesus?

Who in your life has been difficult to love lately? What would it look like to love them like Jesus—sacrificially and unconditionally?

Forever welcomed—that's what we are. As we move through this study, my hope is that we experience the profound depth of God's impartial love. It's a love that actively reaches for us, invites us, and welcomes us every day, even now.

WEEK THREE | IMPARTIAL COMMUNION

Impartial Communion

*God forms relationships, shaping not just individuals
but whole communities that reflect His ways to the world.
His ultimate goal is to draw people into fellowship with Him,
inviting them to know and behold the one true God.
His covenant is more than rules; it's an invitation
into an intimate and personal relationship with Him.*

A Different Kind of Dwelling

From the garden of Eden to the covenants God made with His people, He has always revealed His relentless desire to dwell in relationship with humanity. This week, we come to the tabernacle, a holy dwelling where God's presence resides among His people—an open invitation for sinners to enter into fellowship with Him, though not without its limitations.

It was common in ancient Near Eastern cultures for kings to pitch their tents among their people. But they often remained distant, removed from the daily lives of their subjects.[1]

But God's dwelling among them would be different.

Unlike the stationary temples of surrounding nations, this temporary tent of meeting where God dwelled moved with Israel (Ex. 33:7–11). It was a living, breathing testament to a God who was actively guiding, walking beside, and at times *carrying* His people along (Ex. 13:21–22).

As the Israelites wandered through the wilderness, this tent of meeting proclaimed to them—and the surrounding nations—that their God was not like the silent, indifferent idols of other cultures. He was near, personal, and deeply involved in every step of their journey.

As we reflect on the sacred space of both the tent of meeting and of the fully constructed tabernacle (Ex. 40:1–2) this week, let us marvel at the beauty of God's desire to be with His people. His invitation to commune was not based on their worthiness but on His unchanging, impartial love for sinners who come to Him.

WEEK THREE | DAY ONE

Made in God's Image

Before you begin, ask God to open your eyes to His impartial love, that you may read it, receive it, and respond faithfully.

READ:
Exodus 19:1–6

RECEIVE:
In verse 1, where exactly were God's people when He called them to build a portable tabernacle?

THE WILDERNESS

Some Bible translations call this desert place "the wilderness of Sinai." Far from being a place of abandonment, the desolate becomes a place of intimate relationship.

In the wilderness of Mount Sinai, God commanded His people to build the tabernacle. Not in Egypt, the land they had just left behind (Ex. 12:31–42), nor in the promised land, the destination they were journeying toward (Ex. 3:7–8), but in the wilderness—a barren, fallow place where every step demanded their dependence on Him for survival. It was there, in that empty, uncertain space, that God chose to dwell with His people, teaching them that in even the most desolate of circumstances, His presence is the very thing they need to sustain them and to reflect His image.

FOREVER WELCOMED

God desires to dwell with His people, even in seasons of hardship, transition, waiting, or abundance. What does this reveal about His character?

God meets His people right where they are. Yes, even those places we least expect. *Especially* those places. Even though you may know this truth, do you ever feel like God is nearer to you in seasons of prosperity but distant in times of hardship or struggle? Why or why not?

How does reading that God wants to be with His people, not just in times of prosperity but also in seasons of desolation, realign the way you understand His presence? Complete the sentence:

God, right now, wants to dwell with me in my season of . . .

In this particular season of your life, do you truly believe that God is able to provide everything you need—whether it's direction, clarity, or strength—to serve Him and reflect His character?

☐ Honestly, no, I'm struggling to believe right now.

☐ Yes, I believe, but I need God to help my unbelief at times.

☐ I fully believe, but I desire to grow in even greater faith.

What if our wilderness seasons bring forth a kind of fruit that the barren ground of our insecurities and unanswered questions couldn't possibly predict? And what if our perceived lack leads us to a greater dependence on God's provision? Isn't that the best place to be?

WEEK THREE: IMPARTIAL COMMUNION

Do you believe that you can hope again, even in the wilderness?

Look up the word "tabernacle" in the Background Materials on page 205 and write its meaning in your own words.

Read John 1:14: Who "tabernacled" among us in the New Testament?

God is a God of patterns. What similarities do you notice between the tabernacle built in Exodus and the description of Jesus in John 1:14?

Not only has Jesus come to dwell among His people, but, by the Holy Spirit, God has now come to dwell in His people. What does 1 Corinthians 6:19 then call the bodies of believers?

In the boxes on the following page, draw next to the verse the image that corresponds to what the verse teaches.

Draw a **flame** to represent the Holy Spirit dwelling within you.

Draw a **mirror** to symbolize the transformation taking place as God shapes you into His image.

Draw a **triangle** to represent being God's temple.

You can use more than one symbol for each verse.

Verse	Draw Image
1 Corinthians 6:19–20 *"Do you not know that your bodies are temples of the Holy Spirit, who is in you, whom you have received from God? You are not your own; you were bought at a price. Therefore honor God with your bodies."*	
Ephesians 2:21–22 *"In him the whole building is joined together and rises to become a holy temple in the Lord. And in him you too are being built together to become a dwelling in which God lives by his Spirit."*	
2 Corinthians 6:16 *"What agreement is there between the temple of God and idols? For we are the temple of the living God. As God has said: 'I will live with them and walk among them, and I will be their God, and they will be my people.'"*	

So what does it actually look like to live as someone who's being remade into God's image right here, right now? Whether at work, waiting in the carpool line, or interacting with the cashier at the checkout, there are opportunities in every moment to reflect God's likeness.

Take a moment—right now—to reflect. Write down a few ways your words, actions, and choices in ordinary moments can reflect the transformation of God's presence in the world around you. Look for the ways He not only dwells in you but also is *at work* in you, for good.

1.

2.

3.

RESPOND:

God created us in His image and continues to transform us into His likeness daily; even today, His Spirit is at work—chiseling, refining, and restoring. And one glorious day, believers in Jesus Christ will be fully and perfectly made whole in His image (1 John 3:2). This is the gospel—that even now, in the uncertainty of life, there's a hope that changes everything.

WEEK THREE | DAY TWO

Included in God's Plan

Before you begin, ask God to open your eyes to His impartial love, that you may read it, receive it, and respond faithfully.

READ:
Exodus 25:2–7

RECEIVE:
In these verses, God commands the people to bring an offering for the tabernacle. But notice this: No one is required to give, and no specific amount is mandated. The word "contribution" here can also be understood as an *offering like that of a sacrifice.*[2]

What does this reveal about the heart of God (2 Cor. 9:7)? Check all that apply:

☐ God looks at the heart behind the gift, not just the gift itself.

☐ God desires joyful participation, not begrudging obedience.

☐ God invites humanity into His plans, showing that our contributions truly matter to Him.

Maybe you don't have a "platform," or you feel as though your contributions aren't valuable enough, so you've decided to sit on the sidelines. But God's call to give isn't just for the "platformed." What if it's for you too?

WEEK THREE: IMPARTIAL COMMUNION

In your opinion, how does God's invitation for everyone to give, as their heart prompts, reveal His impartial love?

In contrast, how does our culture (and sometimes even the church) decide who is "worthy" of giving or serving based on status, platform, or appearance?

Imagine being one of the Israelites standing in the wilderness, and you hear Moses' command to bring an offering for the tabernacle. If you chose not to give, what might be the reason? Highlight one that resonates most with where you are today.

- I feel inadequate in what I have to give.

- I feel like my contribution won't make a difference.

- I'm afraid I won't have enough for myself or my family.

- I struggle with knowing whether my gift will be used wisely.

- I feel unqualified to participate in God's work.

- I lack faith because the last time I gave, I didn't feel I received back.

Read the following psalms regarding the tabernacle. Fill in the blanks:

Enter his gates with thanksgiving, _____;
give thanks to him and praise his name. (Ps. 100:4)

78   FOREVER WELCOMED

My soul yearns, even faints, _____;
my heart and my flesh cry out for the living God. (Ps. 84:2)

Better _____ than a thousand elsewhere;
I would rather be a _____my God
than dwell in the tents of the wicked. (Ps. 84:10)

The people of God rejoiced simply in the gift of being able to do what in the outer courts? List a few things from the verses above.

List one way being made aware of the privilege (and gratitude) of entering the outer courts of the tabernacle—God's dwelling place—adds richer meaning to the psalms we so often quote.

Even within the limits of those courts, the hearts of God's people filled with awe and gratitude because the Creator of the universe had made a way for them to draw nearer to His presence.

Now, if the people of Israel found it possible to rejoice in the limited space of the outer courts, how much more should we rejoice today? Through Jesus Christ, we are no longer kept at a distance. We're no longer confined to just the outer courts (Heb. 10:19–22). God has made a way for us to draw so near that His very Spirit now dwells *within* us as believers. The presence of the Creator is not just with us, but in us—never leaving, never departing. We ought to pause and thank God right now for this gift of being included in God's plan.

WEEK THREE: IMPARTIAL COMMUNION

The beauty of our hope as believers is this: *God with us forever.*

The tabernacle in Exodus carried with it a promise of something greater to come. It pointed forward to the day when God's presence would no longer be veiled or confined to a specific space but would, by His Spirit, make His home *in* His people.

How will we respond to His invitation? Read through this list and fill in the empty blanks with the word "come."

To the heartbroken, Jesus says, _____.

To the one overwhelmed by the pressures of this world, Jesus says, _____.

To the one who feels unworthy or unwelcome, Jesus says, _____.

To the one who feels invisible, unnoticed, and alone, Jesus says, _____.

To the one carrying the heavy weight of shame from sin, Jesus says, _____.

To the one battling anxiety and insecurity, Jesus says, _____.

No matter where you've fallen and no matter what you're facing, His invitation remains the same. He calls you to come—just as you are—into His presence. But those who come into His presence never stay the same.

RESPOND:
In light of what we've learned today, read Hebrews 13:15. What would it look like to offer a sacrifice of praise to God this week?

FOREVER WELCOMED

WEEK THREE | DAY THREE

Independent of Culture

Before you begin, ask God to open your eyes to His impartial love, that you may read it, receive it, and respond faithfully.

READ:
Exodus 28:1–5

RECEIVE:
True or False: (Answer as best as you can—even if you're unsure, we'll work through it together.) In Scripture, garments often point us to spiritual truths that prompt us to reflect on our identity in God. Briefly write why you chose your answer or the verses that led you to this answer.

As we observe how clothing is used throughout the Bible, we'll begin to see how the symbolic thread of outer garments relates to the condition of our hearts.[3]

From the detailed priestly garments in Exodus 28:2–3 to the robe of righteousness in Isaiah 61:10 and the white robes of the saints in Revelation 7:9, these vivid images are meant to remind us that believers are called to live set apart lives. We are to be clothed in Christ's righteousness, reflecting God's character in every aspect of our lives.

With the context of living set apart in mind, what do you think are two or three idols in our culture today that tempt us to resist God's call to live according to His Word?

Read Exodus 28:1–5. Take a moment to visualize the garments described in verse 4: the breastpiece, ephod, robe, woven tunic, turban, and sash. If you can, try sketching or drawing these garments based on the descriptions in Exodus 28, or look up images to help you see what they might have looked like.

In Exodus 28:3, who does God command to make the garments for Aaron, the priest? How are these workers described? Write out a list of the unique abilities God says He has given them for this sacred task.

According to Exodus 28:3, why does God distribute these gifts to each person? Who are they ultimately serving?

Read 1 Corinthians 12:4–7. Note how many times the word "same" is used. What patterns from the Old Testament do you notice as it relates to how God distributes spiritual gifts in the New Testament?

Are you tempted to see God's gifts as "better" or "lesser"? Write down one way the truths we've observed can help you view gifts as different parts of a larger whole, each designed to work together for God's greater purpose.

Is there someone now or in the past to whom you are tempted to compare yourself? In what areas?

How might the truth we learned earlier liberate you from the trap of unhealthy comparisons with other believers? Instead of striving to outdo the other, how could it inspire a deeper sense of unity and collaboration as you embrace your specific role and work together for—not apart from—God's glory?

> **TUGGING THE THREADS:** The Hebrew words *'abad* (to serve) and *shamar* (to keep or guard) are like two cords woven throughout the story of Scripture. Together, they describe the holy calling of the priests to serve God with devoted hearts and to guard what is sacred (Num. 3:7–8; 18:5–7).[4] But these words trace even farther back, to the very beginning with Adam and Eve, the first priestly figures. In the garden, they were called to "work" (*'abad*) and to "keep and guard" (*shamar*), reflecting God's heart and fulfilling His will on earth.[5]

Now fast-forward to the New Testament and read 1 Peter 2:9. What spiritual title and role does Scripture give all believers? Fill in the blank:

"A royal _____"

As followers of Jesus, we're invited to mirror God's character to the world by faithfully serving (*'abad*) while also guarding (*shamar*) the sacred responsibilities He has entrusted to us.

Reflect on the responsibilities God has entrusted to you in this season. What are some specific "sacred responsibilities" to which God has called you? Example: Finding opportunities to share the good news of Jesus Christ boldly with fellow parents from my child's school (Matt. 28:19–20). List other ways below:

DON'T LET YOUR GUARD DOWN

The truths we covered today aren't just words written long ago. They're alive and pulsing with relevance for today.

In the New Testament, we are reminded that, as followers of Jesus, we are now the temple of the Holy Spirit (1 Cor. 6:19). We are, in a very real sense, *temple people*. As such, we are called to reflect God's holiness in a world that is drowning in distractions, idols, injustice, and every kind of evil (James 3:16).

We are temple people, living in a specific culture but living independently of it.

Just as the Israelites were called to keep the tabernacle pure, holy, and devoted to God, believers today are called to live in a similar way: set apart, unstained by the world, and wholly devoted to God, reflecting His *dwelling* presence (James 1:27).

But it's not always easy, is it? I know I've *let my guard down* countless times, whether it's giving in to gossip, letting envy creep in, or chasing after things that I think will satisfy but don't—and won't. It's easy to forget who and whose we are in moments of busyness or seasons of hardship. You've likely experienced this too—those times when you just forget that *you* are God's temple.

RESPOND:

Are there areas in your life where you've stopped seeking to live set apart for God? You know, just kind of given up? Do you feel drawn in any area to live comfortably and according to the culture? This could look like slandering others, showing partiality by holding back forgiveness, or seeking approval from people over obedience to God. The list goes on.

Take a moment to pause and reflect. How is God calling you to turn and live according to His truth?

WEEK THREE: IMPARTIAL COMMUNION

If you need a next step, use the words below to guide you in prayer . . .

Father, in view of Your great mercy, I ask that You would help us surrender our lives as a living sacrifice unto You. We desire for our thoughts, actions, and hearts to be holy and pleasing to You. We want everything we do to be a true act of worship.

In Jesus' name, Amen.

WEEK THREE | DAY FOUR

Identity Reimagined

Before you begin, ask God to open your eyes to His impartial love, that you may read it, receive it, and respond faithfully.

READ:

Exodus 32:1–4

RECEIVE:

Exodus 32:1 says that "when the people saw that Moses was _____ _____"

Waiting has a way of exposing what we most deeply believe about our identity.

When Israel gathers together to build the golden calf, what might this reveal about their struggle to believe and embrace their new identity under God?

In seasons of waiting, how are you tempted to take matters into your own hands instead of trusting in God's timing? On the next page, check any or all that apply:

WEEK THREE: IMPARTIAL COMMUNION

- [ ] I'm often tempted to grumble and complain (Ex. 32:1).

- [ ] My instinct is to turn toward lesser gods (e.g., comfort, money, or materialism) (Ex. 32:1).

- [ ] I deny or overlook God's presence with me (Ex. 32:1).

- [ ] I gather others who think like me to construct a different plan than what God revealed to me through His Word (Ex. 32:1).

When we dare to see our identity through God's lens, our view shifts away from false narratives. We begin to see ourselves not as the world sees us—through the lens of fleeting statuses—but as God Himself declares us: beloved, chosen, His. Consider this truth: Even after God's people sinned, God did not give up on them. His presence moved from dwelling in a tent to a fully constructed tabernacle to living within His people through His Spirit (1 Cor. 6:19). God is committed!

How does this reality speak to our shared identity as believers right now? Take a moment to reflect, and check below what resonates most.

- [ ] Understanding that we, as believers, are collectively God's temple stirs a desire within me to pursue unity and impartial love, knowing that together we reflect His presence to the world.

- [ ] I'm beginning to see identity as distinct and sacred, not defined by external achievements, appearances, or the opinions of others but firmly rooted in God's Word.

- [ ] Being His dwelling place inspires me to live with greater purpose and intentionality. Every decision I make—whether in my work, relationships, or the quiet moments of daily life—becomes an opportunity to reflect His glory.

- [ ] This truth challenges me to live set apart, mirroring God's holiness.

- [ ] It reminds me that God's presence is not partial or limited to a specific place or people but is available to anyone, anywhere, who believes.

How does the presence of God among believers serve as a witness that humanity has a new identity?

Fill in the blank using the word bank below (use the Scripture verses in the sentence for help if needed).

word bank: **living, dwelling place, physical**

> It begins with the tent of meeting, then moves to a tabernacle as a _____ dwelling for God's presence among His people in the fully constructed tabernacle (Ex. 40:2; 40:17; 25:8).
>
> Jesus being the _____ presence of God on earth (John 1:14) and culminates in . . .
>
> believers who are now the _____ for God's Spirit (1 Cor. 3:16).

Believer. You are not just someone God loves, you're someone He chooses to live within.

The tabernacle, as we've learned so far in this study, is more than just a physical structure. Every detail reveals God's presence, His invitation into covenant, His provision for sacrifice, and His desire for communion with His people. We've seen this week that the God of the Bible is different from the gods of surrounding nations and invites the Israelites to be different too. To be in God's presence, they need atonement for their sins. And that need would only be fully met in the greater sacrifice to come.

In this story, we see a God who is not content with the brokenness of His people. He is committed to restoring their fractured identity and ours, drawing us back into full communion with Him.

WEEK THREE: IMPARTIAL COMMUNION   89

The tabernacle was never simply just for humanity's sake but literally for God's sake. It was established to declare His glory, to make His presence known, and to reveal His heart—His welcome to the world.

While God has made a place for us, we are to welcome and extend that same love to others. As Christians, how can we guard against the temptation to stay in our own "holy huddle," that cozy little bubble where we only surround ourselves with people who think, believe, and act just like us?

When our identity is reimagined through God's truth, we're reminded of our deeper calling, which is to not just for ourselves but as living temples. Those who are carriers of the very presence of God, vessels of His purpose, and reflections of His love to a broken and dying world.

Consider for a moment what kind of legacy you want to be a part of. Read Revelation 7:9 (in the ESV) and fill in the blanks:

> After this, I looked, and behold, a great multitude that no one could number, from _____, from all _____, standing before the throne and before the Lamb, _____ _____, with palm branches in their hands.

Did you notice John said that he looked, and he saw? He didn't just hear about it or imagine it. John saw colorful distinctions involving people with his own eyes, standing together before the throne of God and the Lamb. This vision was vivid and specific.

Why do you think God chose to show this to John and have him write it down for later believers?

How can this vision inspire us as believers today, especially in light of everything happening in the world? How does it encourage you to pursue unity and to love impartially?

This story? It ends in glory, with God's dwelling forever among His people. A kingdom of priests, face-to-face with Him, united in worship and serving the triune God in unending joy. This is the generous hospitality of God's eternal plan that welcomes sinners home, not for a fleeting moment, but for all eternity. Forever welcomed, forever His.

RESPOND:
Look back on what you've learned this week, the things you circled, marked, or highlighted. As you reflect on God's kingdom that is breaking into earth, how might it change the way you interact with various individuals? What if you were to imagine seeing them again one day in the scene John describes in Revelation 7?

WEEK THREE | DAY FIVE

Impartial Love

Before you begin, ask God to open your eyes to His impartial love, that you may read it, receive it, and respond faithfully.

READ:

Romans 15:4, Exodus 25:8, 31:1–11
Supplemental reading: Revelation 21:1–4, 22–27, 22:1–5

RECEIVE:

We must learn the ancient practice of remembering, of tracing God's fingerprints across the pages of our lives.

We must recount the ways He's carried us . . .

In the Old Testament, God's people found hope by looking back on His past faithfulness and remembering the God who had never failed them. Recalling His mighty works became their strength to trust His promises for the future. Isn't the same true for us today? When we remember how God has been faithful in our past and hold on to His promises for our future, we are living with true hope.

FOREVER WELCOMED

So far this week, how has your heart been moved to see others through God's eyes? In what ways have you been challenged to extend His grace in ways that may feel uncomfortable?

As you reflect on the imagery of accessing God through the outer courts of the tabernacle (Ex. 25:8) and the great multitude of people before the throne of the Lamb (Rev. 7:9), what do you sense God is revealing about His impartial love? Check those that are a fit:

- ☐ Though limited in accessibility, the tabernacle was a reminder that God desires to be near His people, even within the constraints of a fallen world.

- ☐ The multitude before the throne reveals that God's ultimate invitation extends beyond all boundaries to all who seek Him.

- ☐ God's love is a foretaste of heaven where uninterrupted communion will happen with God and one another.

Just as the tabernacle, God's portable dwelling, brought His presence to unexpected places, His love continues to show up through unlikely people, unplanned moments, and unseen spaces where we least expect to encounter Him.

What other patterns of God's impartial love have you noticed in your reading this week?

WEEK THREE: IMPARTIAL COMMUNION

Where have you felt God's love reaching out to you this week? (Example: a verse that spoke directly to your heart, a new insight that deepened your understanding, or a moment during prayer.)

Skim back over Exodus 31:1–11, the passage you read earlier today. Did you sense how these images of God's presence in the tabernacle draw us back to the garden of Eden? How?

Every angle of the tabernacle in Exodus gives us a glimpse of the garden of Eden. Both have an eastward entrance (Ex. 27:13–16), cherubim at the entrance (Ex. 25:18–22; 26:1) and garden imagery (Ex. 25:31–36). Like a mirror reflecting the untarnished beauty of God's original design, these places remind us of God's desire to dwell with His people and to restore what once was.

Read Revelation 22:1–5. Write or draw the elements in this passage that remind you of the garden of Eden as described in Genesis 2:8–10. Where do you see God's restoration?

For all who respond to God's generous invitation, a fully restored Garden awaits, lush with the presence of God and His people, where every longing will find its home (Rev. 22:1–2). It's a place where all that sin has wilted will bloom again.

RESPOND:

Reflect on how God's desire to restore the intimate relationship He shared with humanity in the garden of Eden will culminate in his ultimate plan of restoration (Rev. 21:3–4).

But remember, His desire isn't just for the "someday" of the New Jerusalem; it's for today too.

How do you see God inviting you into fellowship today? Star any of the following:

Through a renewed hunger to spend time in prayer and Scripture.

Through a specific person God has placed in my life to encourage and strengthen me on my faith journey.

Through a recent conviction prompting me to confess sin or surrender an area of my life to Him.

Through seeking to remember His faithfulness in past seasons and trusting His promises for today.

Through a season of challenges, calling me to rely on Him more fully and deepen my faith.

Through opportunities He's opened to serve others and share His love in meaningful ways.

Through the small reassurance of His unconditional and impartial love, meeting me right where I am.

Take a moment to pray a prayer of thanksgiving for the ways God is already working in your life, especially in the areas you've starred. Thank Him for His impartial love that meets you daily, for His constant presence, and for His gentle guidance, even today.

Forever welcomed—that's what we are. As we move through this study, my hope is that we experience the profound depth of God's impartial love. It's a love that actively reaches for us, invites us, and welcomes us every day, even now.

WEEK FOUR | IMPARTIAL CALL

Impartial Call

This six-week journey through Scripture traces the unbroken thread of God's impartial love—an open invitation to all willing to come. Through the voices of the prophets, God calls His people who had broken the covenant to repent and pursue faithfulness through justice and righteousness.

Weekly, we are drawn into walking the cultural landscape, engaging with this holy text, and allowing God's Word to transform our minds and reshape our lives. It's an invitation to receive and embody a love that is wide enough, deep enough, and strong enough to welcome the outsider—including each one of us.

A Message Worth Hearing

The way of life in ancient times was raw and basic. It followed the land's natural cycles and rhythms. Mud, stone, and brick were the materials used for building traditional homes. Many of these included flat roofs, where families gathered to sleep under starlit skies on warm nights. In the cities, towering temples stood as centers of worship, while bustling marketplaces thrived with trade and daily activity.

Can you visualize it?

The spiritual landscape was diverse and dominated by three kinds of religious figures: national gods, worshiped in large, stationary temples within cities; tribal gods, honored at high places by local cult leaders; and family gods, revered as sacred ancestors and protectors.[1]

Unlike Israel, where temple worship was central, most people in surrounding cultures rarely stepped foot in a temple. Instead, they honored family gods or ancestors through daily rituals, often involving small offerings like handmade bread or medicinal herbs together with whispered prayers.[2]

Beneath the rhythms of daily life for someone in the ancient Near East, there was always a quiet, persistent thrumming of fear in the background. So much of life was oriented around not displeasing the gods, who were capricious and prone to fits of rage.[3] The all-consuming presence of empires like Assyria and Babylon hovered with threats of defeat and exile. Political instability hung like a storm cloud, its dark shadow never truly lifting. And even in moments of calm, the restless unease lingered; it was a present reminder of how fragile their lives and nation truly were.

In such times of unease, voices rose to meet the people's desperation. False prophets spoke with charm and certainty, promising peace without the call for repentance. Their words were sweet, but their promises were like a useless bandage—a temporary salve that could not heal the festering wounds of disobedience (1 Kings 18:19–40; Jer. 6:14; Ezek. 13; Acts 13:6–12).

Yet right in the middle of the voices clamoring for the people's attention, the voice of God's true prophets rang out, calling His people to turn back, trust His covenant promises, and remember His unfailing love.

God's message was not always easy, but it was always what His people needed.

Let us lean into the timeless words of the prophets, messages that still speak today to those willing to listen.

They call us back to God's heart, a God whose impartial love invites us to turn away from empty promises and walk in the light of His truth.

May we listen, respond, and find our true rest in Him.

WEEK FOUR | DAY ONE

Made in God's Image

Before you begin, ask God to open your eyes to His impartial love, that you may read it, receive it, and respond faithfully.

READ:
Deuteronomy 18:18–19, Jeremiah 1:9–10

RECEIVE:
We'll go into a detailed description soon, but first, based on the verse you just read, in your own words describe the role and responsibility of a prophet.

Does anything about the prophets' mission or purpose stand out to you or capture your attention?

Read Jeremiah 1:9–10. A prophet is both a receiver and a messenger. As God's representative, the prophet's role is to . . . Circle all that apply.

- guide
- correct
- encourage

God sent as His prophets men and women filled with holy fire and zeal. These messengers were far more than predictors of the future. They were the very voice representing God, speaking truth to culture as social commentators, challenging the status quo, and calling His people back to the consecrated work of living as true reflections of His character. Their words were not designed to draw applause but to draw hearts into alignment with God.

These were His truth-tellers, tasked with piercing through the noise of culture to expose the cracks in the status quo.

Unlike the admiration, fame, and sought-after influence often associated with the role of a prophet or spokesperson in our culture today, the prophets of Scripture walked a path paved with rejection, suffering, and sacrifice. The lives of the prophets were no pedestals of glory. Their obedience led not to comfort but to suffering. Many faced ongoing persecution—some enduring gruesome, tragic deaths—all for the sake of proclaiming a truth that could not be silenced (2 Chron. 24:20–21). All for the steadfast commitment to God's Word and calling.[4]

These men and women stood in the gap, lifting their voices on behalf of the forgotten, the marginalized, and the oppressed (as we'll see). They cried out for sin's walls of division to crumble and for hearts hardened by rebellion to soften. They reminded God's people of their covenantal calling: to dwell with Him and to reflect His glory in a dark and broken world.

Their words still speak today . . . for those willing to listen.

Why do you think God's people needed prophets to continually remind them to reflect His image?

What does this reveal about humanity's deep, often painful tendency to forget God's commands and drift from His ways, even when we are aware of the consequences?

This week, pay close attention to how many prophets delivered similar messages in different places, whether they lived in the same era or were separated by centuries.

Remember how we've been tracing God's patterns? It's one of my favorite things about His Word. It transcends time, crosses cultural divides, and speaks with a relevance and power that is both timeless and timely. His truth isn't confined by geography or history. Hear me: It is sufficient for every moment, always fresh in its application, and always enough for what we need. Thank You, Jesus!

Read Micah 6:8. Write out God's expectations listed for His people:

To _____

To _____

To _____

The words of the prophet Micah capture the heart of God's message to His people through the prophets we'll read about this week: to act justly (with fairness and standing for what is right), to love mercy (showing kindness and favor to those who may not deserve it), and to walk humbly (living in dependence on God and valuing others above yourself).

Take a moment to pause and reflect. Ask yourself: Which of these three areas challenges me the most? Write down what comes to mind.

For some, justice may feel intimidating because it requires us to stand up for what's right, even when it's inconvenient or uncomfortable. For others, mercy can stretch us in different ways, asking us to extend grace when it feels undeserved (maybe you're thinking about a situation right now). And humility, well, that one touches us all. It calls us to lay down our pride, surrender control, and walk in complete dependence on God as we seek to value others above ourselves.

Read Psalm 89:14 in the New King James Version of the Bible, and fill in the blank:

Righteousness _____;
_____ and truth go before Your face. (NKJV)

True or False: God's justice and mercy are two sides of the same coin, both reflected in His dealings with His people throughout the Bible. Briefly explain why you chose your answer.

Take your time as you read through the following verses spoken by the prophets, paying close attention to the nature and character of God's impartial love.

Look up the following verses and write them down:

Isaiah 1:17 —

Micah 6:8 —

Jeremiah 22:3 —

Zechariah 7:9–10 —

Now circle or underline any descriptions of God's character in the verses above.

Do you notice any repetitive themes involving God's impartial love present in these verses? List below.

Complete the following sentences. I see the image of a God

who_____.

I can reflect this image by_____.

Why do you think God draws near to those who are physically desperate, emotional dependent, and spiritually destitute or deprived?

God draws near to us too. List one way the physical desperation of the poor, needy, and destitute mirror the spiritual desperation we all experience.

As we'll continue to observe throughout this week, God's prophets consistently called God's people to reflect His heart toward the marginalized and overlooked. Who are the hurting, forgotten, or invisible people in your life that God's been nudging you to notice?

RESPOND:
Sister, God came for them, but He also came for you.

- Do you feel spiritually marginalized by your struggles with sin?

- Do you feel impoverished by your past or burdened by decisions you've made, even today?

- Has anxiety, fear, or worry been holding you captive and leaving you feeling destitute?

Be encouraged. God came for the poor—the physically and spiritually poor—to bring hope. What if the very places where you feel empty and unworthy are the places where God longs to pour out His impartial love and grace? Can you trust that the God who hears the cries of the poor and defends the helpless also sees your silent struggles, your deepest spiritual need?

How does being reminded of this truth challenge the way you approach God in your moments of desperation?

As you see God as the One who welcomes your weakness and meets you in your most fragile moments, it's not just that He stirs courage within you. He also causes it to flow out of you toward others.

WEEK FOUR | DAY TWO

Included in God's Plan

Before you begin, ask God to open your eyes to His impartial love, that you may read it, receive it, and respond faithfully.

READ:
Hebrews 1:1–2

RECEIVE:
According to Hebrews 1:1, in the past God spoke to our ancestors through whom and how?

As we see in the chart on the following page, the prophets carried God's timeless messages across generations, speaking to diverse places and circumstances— sometimes even at the same time. Take a look at the chart below and look up the verses. Which theme(s) and verses intrigue you the most? Why?

Theme	Prophets Who Spoke Them
Judgment	Ezekiel 7:3–4, Jeremiah 25:4–6, Amos 5:18–20, Ezekiel 18:30, Hosea 4:1–2, Jonah 3:4, Ezekiel 7:5–6
Repentance and Righteousness	Amos 5:14–15, Isaiah 1:16–17, Jeremiah 4:1–4, Ezekiel 18:30
Renewal	Isaiah 1:18, Joel 2:12–13, Isaiah 55:6–7
Hope and Restoration	Jeremiah 29:11, Isaiah 1:18, Isaiah 40:1–2, Hosea 14:4–7
Social Injustice	Micah 6:8, Isaiah 1:17, Amos 5:11–12
Imagery or Parables	Hosea 1:2, Ezekiel 4:1–3, Jeremiah 13:1–11
Idolatry	Isaiah 44:9–11, Jeremiah 10:1–5, Ezekiel 14:3–6
False Prophets	Jeremiah 23:16, Ezekiel 13:2–3, Micah 3:5–7
Prayers and Intercession	Exodus 32:11, Daniel 9:3–5, Jeremiah 14:7–9
God's Sovereignty	Jeremiah 32:17, Isaiah 45:5–7, Daniel 4:34–35
Individual and Collective Sin	Isaiah 58:6–7, Ezekiel 18:30–32, Micah 6:6–8

Throughout the prophets' writings, we can trace recurring themes: the weight of judgment, the snare of idolatry, the cries against social injustice, the ever-present danger of false teaching. Yet woven like a golden thread through their urgent pleas was also a constant hope.

As you read through this list, why do you think that, despite so much judgment pronounced, there might also be hope and a welcome of restoration?

God's hope, like rain, falls on the parched ground of hearts so that those He calls can carry and pour out His impartial love to others . . .

Each prophet had his or her own distinct style, unique gifts, and personal way of expressing God's message; yet every one of them was led by the same Spirit. I love how God works this way, don't you?

Recall the verse we read earlier, Hebrews 1:1. Paraphrase it in your own words.

How do you see God's heart, not only in the messages He delivers but in the diverse voices He calls to share them (Heb. 1:1; 2 Peter 1:21)?

What does this reveal about His character and His deep desire to include all kinds of people—people like (and not like) you and me—to accomplish His good and perfect plans? Check any that apply.

It shows me that God values diversity in His messengers. God chose prophets from all walks of life—rich and poor, young and old, those with influence and those without, reminding me that He doesn't limit His work to any one type of person.

It shows me that God uses our unique gifts and personalities. Some prophets, like Isaiah, spoke with poetic beauty, and others, like Jeremiah, delivered God's truth, weeping with boldness.

It shows me that God's message is for everyone, and He empowers us to share it. Even with their different styles and voices, the prophets were united in one purpose: to proclaim God's truth.

It shows me that God can redeem anyone for His purpose. Many of the prophets were unlikely candidates—people whom the world might overlook or reject—yet God called and used them powerfully.

It shows me that God's work is bigger than any one person. Each prophet had a unique role, but all were part of a larger story of God's forever welcome into redemption.

It's the tapestry of redemption. Are you starting to see the intricate patterns God is weaving through every part of Scripture?

Read Isaiah 55:1–7. What is the direction the Lord gives through Isaiah in the first half of verse 1?

Isaiah 55 is often called a chapter of hope, nestled near the close of what biblical scholars name the "Book of Comfort" (Isa. 40–55).[5] Here, in chapter 55, the prophet Isaiah transitions from the weight of judgment to the offerings of hope and restoration. It is a passage with a welcome—God's voice speaking through Isaiah, calling His people and the nations to come, to turn to Him for redemption, and to find healing in Him.

This chapter demonstrates God's inclusive plan, not just for then but for now. Even today, God's mercy, grace, and salvation are rolled out before all who seek Him.

So come, Isaiah says, and taste the goodness of God . . .

Now write down the last line of Isaiah 55:1. List out the qualifications for coming.

The invitation is extended to those "who have *no* money," to those who feel they have nothing to offer and nothing of value to bring.

Wait a minute—life and redemption offered freely? That's a reality that feels almost too good to be true in our culture, where value is measured by price tags and inclusion often comes with strings attached.

What does this teach us about God's willingness to welcome and bless those who feel inadequate or empty-handed?

How does this invitation turn our typical view of inclusion upside down?

In what ways do you feel spiritually or emotionally empty right now? Where does your soul feel dry? Write it down.

Take a deep breath and lean into the truth that God sees it. He knows it. And He's inviting you to come to Him.

If the only thing you take away from today is the habit of bringing your emptiness to God again and again, then, sister, you've received more than enough.

God's Word assures us that He has always been ready to pour out His abundance on all who come—not with pretense or grasping at self-sufficiency, but with hearts laid bare and hands open wide to receive His welcome, His way. This is the God who meets us in our need, and who fills us with more than we could ever imagine or dare to ask.

I dare you . . . come to Him and stay a while.

Grab hold of what truth(s) you need today:

- God satisfies the thirsty (Isa. 55:1).

- God exchanges weariness for rest (Matt. 11:28).

- God provides for the needs of His children (Phil. 4:19).

- God continuously draws near to the brokenhearted (Ps. 34:18).

RESPOND:
God's invitation is for the thirsty, for the hungry, for those who have a longing for something this temporal life can never satisfy. How will you take a step toward this living water today (Isaiah 55:1)?

"Come, buy, and eat without money and without cost" (Isa. 55:1). There's a table set for the unworthy.

Will you come?

WEEK FOUR: IMPARTIAL CALL   113

WEEK FOUR | DAY THREE

Independent of Culture

Before you begin, ask God to open your eyes to His impartial love, that you may read it, receive it, and respond faithfully.

READ:

Jeremiah 1:1–10

RECEIVE:

Today is going to be a little longer to give our study of one prophet its due. If you need to break up the lesson into more than one day, that's okay. Remember, this isn't about checking off a box or racing through the material—the goal is to know and love God more.

Jeremiah is known as the "weeping prophet." He walked faithfully in obedience to God through one of the darkest periods in Israel's history. It was a time of spiritual decay, pervasive social injustice, and intense political instability. God's covenant people had veered far off course, driven by the idolatrous practices of the nations around them.

The prophets remind us that faithfulness isn't always met with applause.

114　FOREVER WELCOMED

Based on Jeremiah 1:4–10, did Jeremiah have any merit, status, or good works that made him worthy of God's choice?

What can we learn from God's reassurance to Jeremiah about His presence and provision (see Jer. 1:8)?

Jeremiah's role was to be the voice of Yahweh, calling the people back to their true identity and calling. Despite all of Jeremiah's warnings and cries for repentance, the people of Judah turned a deaf ear, hardening their hearts against God's message and His messenger (Jer. 23:16–22; 28:1–17).

I want you to read this aloud, twice: And yet, Jeremiah kept going, his eyes fixed on God, though at times, they were filled with tears. Jeremiah was fully committed to his prophetic mission, even as it led him into rejection, sorrow, and deep personal cost—because God was with him. *God was with him.*

Pause and reflect. Has there ever been a time you experienced a unique reassurance from God even in the midst of hardship or great difficulty? How did you know it was God?

How did His reassurance encourage you and maybe even those around you during this time?

Time and again, God's promise of His presence and provision accompany His call.

Look up the following verses observing how each prophet called by God responds. Write down what they said.

Look up Exodus 4:10	What is Moses' response?
Look up Jeremiah 1:6	What is Jeremiah's response?
Look up Isaiah 6:5	What is Isaiah's response?
Look up Ezekiel 3:1	What is Ezekiel's response?

What do these verses consistently reveal about God's faithfulness in equipping and strengthening His servants?

As we continue our study today, you may be surprised by what you discover. Though prophets like Jeremiah spoke thousands of years ago, their words still cut through time, piercing directly into the heart of our culture . . . even today. Truth has a way of doing that. It transcends not just centuries but circumstances, sometimes even reaching right to our own doorsteps and bringing conviction when we least expect it.

Read the following verses and fill in the blanks:

Jeremiah 6:13 (CSB) – "For from the least to the greatest of them, _____ _____; and from prophet to priest, _____.

Jeremiah 14:14 (ESV) – "And the LORD said to me: '_____ _____. I did not send them, nor did I command them or speak to them. They are prophesying to you a lying _____ _____.'"

Jeremiah 23:16 (ESV) – "Thus says the LORD of hosts: 'Do not listen to the words of the prophets who prophesy to you, _____ _____ _____.'"

Jeremiah 23:21–22 (ESV) – "I did not send the prophets, yet they ran; I did not speak to them, yet they prophesied. _____

_____

_____

_____."

In Week One we learned that God is impartial, even in His judgment of sin. Look closely at these verses. How do you see God's impartial love spoken in truth?

Which characteristics of false prophets do you notice being exposed? What are some of the deceptive promises that sound so appealing?

And as you read, ask yourself: Do any of these lies sound familiar to the messages I'm choosing to take in today?

Read 2 Peter 2:1 and 2 Timothy 4:3–4. Is false teaching something that only existed in the days of the Old Testament prophets like Jeremiah? Or has it woven its way through history, threading into every generation—even ours today?

God's people wanted the *influence* of false prophets more than the *truth* of God's Word. God's people wanted the *comfort* of false prophets more than the *conviction* of God's Word. They preferred prophets whose messages aligned with *their desires* and encouraged *conformity to the norms* of the surrounding culture.

And so, these prophets told the people *what they wanted to hear*, leading them further away from the path of true repentance and restoration.

Based on the verses we just read, it becomes clear how false teachers draw people away from the call to live "set apart"— distinct and holy unto God. They are thought leaders, not truth speakers; they cater to the culture, encouraging compromise where God has called for faithfulness. Circle or highlight any and all that ring true . . .

False teachers can be:

- Partial toward teaching that God guarantees wealth, health, and success to those who have enough faith, promoting a transactional view of God and distorting God's character to a cosmic vending machine.

- Partial toward power and influence, favoring those with wealth, power, or those in VIP positions of spiritual authority. They perpetuate the false idea that God's favor is tied to position rather than humility.

- Partial toward comforting passages, they cling to feel-good promises, conveniently ignoring the harder truths of Scripture that call for repentance and denial of self.

- Partial toward sin by refusing to confront blatant sins of the culture. They preach messages that tickle the ears (2 Tim. 4:3).

True teachers and prophets don't mince words, and *neither should Christ's followers*. The Word of God does not make room for half-truths or sugarcoated messages that leave gaps in the truth. The stakes for souls are too high.

These partialities misrepresent God and lead people to a counterfeit version of faith, one that aligns with the world's standards rather than God's. Jeremiah's warnings remind us to stay grounded in the full truth of God's Word and live as His holy, set-apart people.

RESPOND:

Take a moment to reflect on how religious beliefs can sometimes become entangled with the sway of culture in an effort to gain popularity or approval. Think about how faith is sometimes diluted to blend into the contours of societal norms, how the hard edges of biblical truth can be softened to avoid offense and maintain influence.

Check any or all examples below that you've been tempted by in our modern context.

☐ Messages that appeal to human desires rather than pursuing God's righteousness.

☐ Teachings that mix biblical truth with worldly ideologies and false beliefs.

☐ Ideas that prioritize self-gratification, comfort, or worldly success over spiritual growth.

☐ Messages that create division or confusion within the body of Christ.

☐ "Me-centered" theology that spreads rapidly and weakens the faith of believers.

☐ Teachings that reject accountability and godly authority.

Reflect on this day and take an honest assessment. Is there a lie that you have bought into, allowing it to shape your thinking or actions more than the truth of God's Word? How is God calling you to turn and walk in biblical truth— reflecting God within the culture while remaining independent of its beliefs?

Living within the culture while remaining independent of its influence is a tough, often unpopular, and narrow road to walk. So, how do we do it? How can we begin to discern the false teachings of our day?

It all starts with awareness—turning to the true story of Scripture and letting it shape how we see the world around us. When we anchor ourselves in the truth of God's Word, we sharpen our spiritual senses, guiding us to discern truth from falsehood—just as you are doing through this study.

WEEK FOUR | DAY FOUR

Identity Reimagined

Before you begin, ask God to open your eyes to His impartial love, that you may read it, receive it, and respond faithfully.

READ:
Ezekiel 1:1–3, Ezekiel 36:22–26

RECEIVE:
Even as the prophet Jeremiah wept over Jerusalem's rebellion and coming destruction, God had raised up Ezekiel, another prophet hundreds of miles away in Babylon.

Though their lives never really intersected, both prophets carried the same God-given burden, speaking God's truth during some of Israel's darkest seasons.

Jeremiah remained in Jerusalem, the heart of Judah, as he painfully watched the city he loved crumble under the weight of sin (Jer. 38:28; Lam. 1:1–4).

Ezekiel, on the other hand, was already in Babylon among the first wave of exiles. Far from the familiar everyday rhythms of his homeland, Ezekiel's prophetic ministry began among the broken and displaced; a people grieving the loss of everything they'd known. Like Jeremiah, Ezekiel spoke of judgment for sin, yet also like Jeremiah, his words carried a thread of hope. He prophesied about a future day when God would return His people back to their land and provide them with new hearts and restore their covenant relationship with Him (Ezek. 11:17–20; 36:24–28; 37).

122   FOREVER WELCOMED

Even in the ashes of exile, God's invitation to be restored was still extended.

According to what we read, Ezekiel's ministry didn't begin within the familiar walls of Jerusalem's temple. Instead, it began where?

> *Ezekiel was called to speak God's truth*
> *in a place that seemed far from holy.*

How could Ezekiel speak God's truth in such loss? Read the following verse and fill in the final line of Ezekiel 1:3: "There the hand of the _____."

Circle what you think Ezekiel needed to root his identity in to faithfully fulfill his calling.

- His circumstances

- His calling

- His approval given by man

- His relationship with God

- His skill sets and abilities

It was in that exile, far from everything Ezekiel had known, that God still used him mightily. It was in exile that Ezekiel experienced God's presence, which was not confined to a place.

And it was in exile that God gave Ezekiel visions of His glory, messages of His mission, and promises of restoration. It was in the raw, unsanitized pain of exile that God's power shone through Ezekiel's ministry, reminding His people—and us—that no place is too broken for God to work. None. God is able to give His people an identity reimagined anywhere they find themselves.

Read Ezekiel 3:1–3. What pattern do you notice in how God calls His prophets?

Now, I don't want you to miss this. Take a second to visualize what is being described in Ezekiel 3:1–3. The scroll, folded upon itself, covered in God's very words, is handed to Ezekiel, not to simply read, not to just hold, but to *eat*. To take it in fully, to let it penetrate, and become part of him. And the taste? Sweet as honey.

If the message Ezekiel received included a word of judgment, how could it be sweet as honey?

Ezekiel wasn't just bringing bitter news; he was also delivering God's invitation for transformation. It was a message infused with the sweetness of God's truth.

Even when God's Word carries tough messages and delivers hard truths, it's ultimately (if not immediately) sweet, because it has the power to bring life where there was none.

Before Ezekiel could speak God's Word, he had to fully consume it, internalize it, and allow it to become a part of him. In other words, He had to let it transform his heart before it could shape his message.

What does this reveal about the irreplaceable role of God's Word in preparing us for God's work?

Read John 15:5. What parallel can you draw between Ezekiel's call to internalize God's Word and Jesus' call to believers in John 15:5?

God's command to Ezekiel is to_____ (Ezek. 3:1–3).

Jesus calls believers to_____ (John 15:4–7).

In Ezekiel 36, God says He will regather the Israelites from the nations where they've been scattered and restore them to their land. But this promise is about so much more than returning to a geographic location; it's an invitation from God to experience true wholeness.

Read Ezekiel 36:22–23 (ESV). Why does the Lord say that He is about to act? Fill in the blanks:

"It is not for _____

_____ but for _____ which you have

profaned among the nations where you have gone."

God's people are recipients of His grace and also vessels of His glory. Their new identity reflects God's desire to restore His name and pour out His glory *through* them. God's people are living testimonies—temple people—displaying that God's power to restore isn't limited to "us" but extends through us to the world. Through them, the nations will encounter God's wide welcome.

Look briefly at Ezekiel 36:26, which speaks of an *identity reimagined*, a transformation in which God promises to remove their "heart of stone" and replace it with a "heart of flesh." What do you think it really means to have a "heart of stone" today? Circle any or all . . .

- Resistance to God's authority, His will, His Word

- Unwillingness to surrender or choosing delayed obedience

- Indifference toward God and others

- Clinging to traditions or idols over genuine worship and devotion

A "heart of stone" is hardened, unyielding, and closed off to the life-changing power of God. But a "heart of flesh"? It is soft, responsive, and ready to be molded by God's Spirit.

RESPOND:

Reflect for a moment. Where might God be inviting you to surrender your hardness of heart? Are there areas where you're resisting God's will, ignoring His Spirit, or allowing your heart to grow cold toward Him?

Hosea 10:12, the prophet urges us: "Break up your unplowed ground; for it is time to seek the LORD, until he comes and showers his righteousness on you." God offers to take their (and our) cold, unyielding hearts of stone and replace them with soft, tender hearts of flesh that are open, alive, and filled with His Spirit. This is a transformation that redefines identity. This is a renewal of relationship that gives us new hearts.

WEEK FOUR | DAY FIVE

Impartial Love

Before you begin, ask God to open your eyes to His impartial love, that you may read it, receive it, and respond faithfully.

READ:
Matthew 5:17 (see below)

"Do not think that I [Jesus] have come
to abolish the Law or the Prophets;
I have not come to abolish them but to fulfill them."
(Matt. 5:17)

RECEIVE:
Answer the following by writing True or False:

While the prophets served as vessels for God's Word, delivering His truth to the people, Jesus is the very Word of God made flesh: the living embodiment of His truth.

The prophets pointed to the coming Messiah—Jesus Christ, the One who would not only speak God's promises but also completely fulfill them.

Reflect on the prophets from our study this week; where have you been surprised by God's impartial love?

What are two timeless truths proclaimed by the prophets that still resonate powerfully in addressing the challenges and issues of our culture today?

Was there a theme from this week that resonated most deeply with you? What about that theme made it feel personal and real?

RESPOND:

As you sit with and process all we've walked through this week . . . what might be holding you back from fully accepting God's invitation to come just as you are, even today? Highlight any or all options you believe to be true.

- **Pride:** I believe I can handle life on my own without needing God's help.

- **Lack of understanding:** I don't know how to approach God or have a relationship with Him.

- **Busyness:** I am too distracted to prioritize time with God.

- **Doubt:** I am uncertain about God's existence, love, or ability to forgive me.

- **Fear of judgment:** I worry that God will reject or punish me for what I've done wrong.

- **Fear of change:** I fear that coming to God will require me to give up certain behaviors or lifestyles.

- **Anger or resentment:** I feel hurt by unanswered prayers and sometimes blame God.

- **Pain or suffering:** I feel abandoned by God in times of hardship, which makes it hard to approach Him.

- **Feeling spiritually dry:** I feel a sense of distance or disconnection from God in this season.

What small, intentional steps can you take to move beyond the obstacles holding you back? Sometimes it's not about giant leaps but the small, faithful choices that lead us closer into God's invitation. Consider what shifts in mindset, action, or prayer might help you overcome these barriers. Some examples might include...

- Leaning into God's Word and living in obedience

- Relying more on God's strength instead of my own

- Seeking out and surrounding myself with a godly community

- Recalling God's faithfulness through daily gratitude

Write your own answer in response here:

Forever welcomed—that's what we are. As we move through this study, my prayer is that we feel the depth of God's impartial love—a love that reaches out to each of us who falls short and draws us close to His compassion, grace, and abounding love. This love is personal; it reaches for us, invites us, and welcomes us every day.

It's a love that calls you by name. No matter where you find yourself today, God is inviting you to come close.

You are welcomed.

The Dark Silence Before Dawn

Four hundred years of silence.

Between the Old Testament and the New.

No new prophet. No new word. Just the echo of ancient promises
through generations, faint but unbroken.

But God's silence never means God's inactive.

Even in the quiet, He was moving, threading His purposes
through the tapestry of history, fulfilling prophecies spoken long ago.

God's people watched and waited, longing in expectation for God to show up,

yearning for His voice to break through the quiet.

And then—after 400 years of silence, 400 years of longing—God showed up.

God broke through the silence. He heard the cries of His people,
and He answered with a baby's cry in Bethlehem—Savior, clothed in humanity,
wrapped in the fragile frame of a King.

And won't this same God who pierced the silence then do it again?

Won't He come once more for His people: those who still wait, still long,
still wander in a world that feels foreign and fractured?

Won't He rend the heavens once more to make all things new?

He will.

He is the answer to the 400-year ache and the answer to every ache we carry still.

— OGHOSA IYAMU

WEEK FIVE | IMPARTIAL CHRIST

Impartial Christ

*From the womb to the tomb, Jesus perfectly embodied impartial love.
Throughout His ministry, He broke down the walls that divided
God from humanity and people from each other.
One-third of Jesus' teachings were stories centered on
a powerful theme: God's radical welcome of the unlikely,
regardless of their status or past.*

Torn Between Cultures

Days began long before the sun rose above the horizon, with residents stirred awake by the demands of agrarian life. Homes were built using clay with straw or stone, and many residents had a vine in their backyards for the harvest of grapes to make wine. In first-century Palestine, families prepared for long days of toil. Daily activity included plowing fields, building in carpentry sheds, or trading in crowded marketplaces, bargaining deals and selling goods.

Oils being extracted from olives intertwined with the air's scents of fish, spices, and fresh produce. Different merchants called out to those passing by, their voices rising louder than the bleating of livestock and the steady shuffle of feet.[1] Day in and day out, the Roman soldiers walked the streets with an ever-watchful eye, enforcing the emperor's law with authority.

Roman dominance came with the pressures of pagan practices and polytheistic worship, which conflicted with the true Jewish faith.[2] This divide between the two worlds created major divisions among Jewish communities. Many sects sought their own way of navigating the challenges of life under Roman rule. Pharisees clung to the law, seeking to guard their generational traditions. Those called Sadducees used political power to maintain their influence. The Zealots, on the other hand, were known to resist Roman rule—some in secret, others in open rebellion, retreating to the wilderness as they awaited the promised Messiah.

WEEK FIVE: IMPARTIAL CHRIST

Many living in this climate felt trapped—torn between cultures, political alliances with empires, and differing religious convictions.

Jewish people in the first century experienced life as a fragile balance; they were constantly strained between the desire to remain faithful and honor their heritage and the harsh realities of Roman rule that came with doing so. The gap between the wealthy elite and the ordinary people grew wider each day. Relentless taxation combined with temple tithes forced farmers, laborers, and fishermen to struggle to survive, often leaving them with little, and sometimes nothing, to feed their families.

And yet, as the weight of darkness further pressed in on this world, the Light of the World was drawing near, impartial love wrapped in human flesh. *Immanuel*— God with us—was living proof of God's desire to dwell among His people, to bring hope to the weary, and to invite them into a kingdom where they would be *forever welcomed*.

WEEK FIVE | DAY ONE

Made in God's Image

Before you begin, ask God to open your eyes to His impartial love, that you may read it, receive it, and respond faithfully.

READ:

Genesis 1:26–27, Philippians 2:6–8

RECEIVE:

As we begin this week, let's pause and behold Jesus Christ. He's not a figure or a character in a story. *He is the story.* Our Savior, Redeemer, Lord, and King.

According to your reading, fill in the blanks:

Genesis 1:27 — "So God created mankind in his own image, _____ _____ . . ."

Philippians 2:6–8 — "Who, being in very nature God, did not consider equality with God something to be used to his own advantage; rather, he made himself nothing by taking the very nature of a servant, _____ _____. And being found in _____, he humbled himself . . ."

WEEK FIVE: IMPARTIAL CHRIST

Genesis 1:27 reveals that God created mankind in His own image. Philippians 2:6–8 says Jesus Christ, though fully God, took on the nature of a servant, being made in the likeness of whom?

Read Colossians 1:15–20 and fill in the blank:

Jesus is called the "image _____."

What kind of God stoops way down low, stepping into the mess and mire of humanity? A God who comes near, not because He has to, but because His love doesn't allow Him to stay distant.

How does God the Son, taking on human form in the person of Jesus Christ (Phil. 2:6–8) reveal God's unchanging desire to reconcile humanity to Himself?

Since humanity failed to reflect the image of God, God took on the image of man to show us how to perfectly reflect Him.

We've been slowly uncovering throughout this study how, from the very beginning, God created humanity with a purpose: to reflect His character and partner with Him in shaping His world. But instead, humanity chose independence, allowing sin to fracture that reflection. Yet even in our brokenness, God's grace and impartial love remained within reach. God didn't just send help; He Himself *became* the help and the way (John 14:6). Jesus is the ultimate example of what humanity was created to be (Rom. 8:29; Col. 1:15).

Read 1 Corinthians 15:45. What does it tell us about the last Adam in comparison to the first?

Because of His life, death, and resurrection, we no longer have to be bound by the chains of sin and death. Jesus made a way for us to be restored and transformed. But this is an invitation, a gift you must choose to receive . . .

If you've never placed your faith in Jesus Christ, take this moment to do so. You will find a prompt and prayer to walk through on page 201.

> **TUGGING THE THREADS:** In the Old Testament, ancient Near Eastern cultures saw the womb as central to a woman's identity.[3] Being fertile gave you honor and legacy.[4] This was in many ways a culture of desired and sought-after fertility. Many cultures in the Mesopotamia region paid homage to fertility gods and goddesses, practicing cultic rituals for the purpose of fertility. This is the narrative that surrounded the Israelites and that was practiced by the surrounding cultures.

In light of what we just learned, how do you see the significance when you consider both the curse (Gen. 3:16) and the miracle of salvation through the womb in Scripture (Luke 1:42)?

Look up Luke 1:30–31. What message do you think God might have been communicating by choosing Jesus to enter the world through a womb?

In some ways, the womb is a paradox.
It's a place where the promise of both pain and hope can coexist.

The first thing Jesus redeems when He comes to earth is the womb. The womb, marked by the sting of death is through Jesus Christ bringing forth the ultimate source of life.

Were you surprised to learn that the first thing Jesus redeems when He comes to earth is the womb? Why did you react the way you did?

In what ways can Mary be seen then as a "new Eve"[5] in the story of salvation? Mark all that apply:

- ☐ Mary's obedience plays an important role in birthing God's plan of redemption and the restoration of humanity through Jesus Christ (Luke 1:38).

- ☐ Through Mary, the promise of the "seed" of the woman in Genesis 3:15 is fulfilled, as Jesus triumphs over sin and death, "crushing the head of the serpent" (Gen. 3:15).

- ☐ The birth of Jesus marks the beginning of a new humanity, just as Eve was called the mother of all living (2 Cor. 5:17).

- ☐ Eve doubted God's Word in the garden, and Mary believed God's Word, demonstrating faith and trust (Luke 1:45).

- ☐ Eve's decision led to separation from God, while Mary's decision opened the way for reconciliation to God through Jesus Christ (2 Cor. 5:18).

- ☐ As Eve's sin ushered in death, Mary welcomed in the One who would bring eternal life (John 11:25).

Before we respond, let's reflect on the following truths from Scripture about the image of Christ and what it means for our lives today:

Look up the following verses (I used the NIV) and fill in the blanks . . .

Romans 8:29 — Believers are being conformed into the image of

_____.

2 Corinthians 3:18 — Believers are being transformed into the

_____ through the Holy Spirit.

Colossians 3:10 — Believers are continuously being renewed in knowledge in the image of _____.

Ephesians 4:22–24 — Believers are called to "put on" the new self, which is created _____ in righteousness and holiness.

Philippians 3:20–21 — But our citizenship is in heaven. And we eagerly await a Savior from there, the Lord _____, who, by the power that enables Him to bring everything under His control, will transform our lowly bodies so that they will be _____ glorious body.

Even on our hardest days or in seasons that seem like they might break us, the Spirit is steadily at work, forming us into the image of Christ, often in ways we cannot yet see.

God is weaving every piece of our story—even the broken, frayed, and painful strands—into His grand narrative of redemption.

Nothing will go wasted in His sovereign hands. So hold fast, even if your grip is wet with tears. Glory is coming.

RESPOND:

He is the God who chose both the cradle and the cross to bring us near . . .

As we close today, read through the names of Jesus below. Read them slowly. Say them aloud if you can. As you do, let each name of Jesus preach to your soul who He truly is.

He is . . .

- Healer (Isa. 53:5)

- Helper (Heb. 2:18)

- Shelter (Ps. 32:7)

- Shepherd (John 10:11)

- Protector (Ps. 18:2)

- Immanuel, God with us (Matt. 1:23)

- Prince of Peace (Isa. 9:6)

- Redeemer (Job 19:25)

Pause for a moment and let those names settle. Resist the urge to rush past them. In the stillness, ask the Holy Spirit to continue to reveal Jesus in a fresh, personal, and transformative way as you move through the remainder of this study.

How might trusting in Jesus Christ, the One who broke the ultimate curse of sin to reconcile and restore, shift the way you approach God in the broken and unfinished areas of your life?

WEEK FIVE | DAY TWO

Included in God's Plan

Before you begin, ask God to open your eyes to His impartial love, that you may read it, receive it, and respond faithfully.

READ:
Matthew 1:1–17

RECEIVE:
The writings of Matthew in the New Testament were created with a Jewish audience in view.[6] He strategically ties the Old and New Testaments together, pointing to Jesus Christ as the long-awaited fulfillment of prophecies the Jewish people had clung to for generations.

Right from the opening verses, Matthew traces Jesus' lineage straight back to Abraham and David, reminding his readers that this isn't a brand-new story. It's the continuation of the one God has been telling all along. Jesus Christ is the climax of Israel's history—and ours too!

In Matthew 1:1–17, what phrase do you notice being repeated? Write it down.

What literary break in expectation do you notice in verse 16?

WEEK FIVE: IMPARTIAL CHRIST

Where do you see God's attribute of impartiality as you read through this Jewish genealogy? (Refer to "Impartiality" in the Background Materials on page 206 for guidance.)

In our culture, we meticulously craft resumes to impress. We want to showcase our achievements, skills, and all the ways we've proven ourselves. We want others to see, without a shadow of a doubt, that we're the right person for the job.

For the Jewish people, a genealogy served a similar purpose. While we might skim over family trees and read just a list of names, to them, it was far more. It was a declaration of their identity. It spoke of where they came from and to whom they belonged.[7]

If not a genealogy or resume, what are you tempted to showcase as proof of your own worthiness?

It was not uncommon for kings like Herod the Great and other high nobles to selectively edit their genealogies to remove parts that didn't fit the desired public image.[8] Just like we often do today, they wanted a version of themselves that excluded failure, shame, and anything that might hurt their reputation.

But Jesus? His genealogy is nothing like we'd imagine. He is perfect, though His genealogy is not your typical "airbrushed" version of perfection. Matthew begins his gospel with a family tree that's full of "*really? . . . him . . . her?*" moments. Some of the names on this list are tied to messy, often scandalous stories. The list includes murderers, idolaters, prostitutes, Gentiles, and women (not the best status at the time). These are people who would never make the cut in a typical royal genealogy. But as we read these names and stories, we can almost hear the gospel being preached,[9] showing us that no one is beyond the reach of God's grace.

Read the following verses from Matthew 1 and identify the woman mentioned in each:

Read Matthew 1:3. Who is the woman mentioned?

What is one thing we learn about her in Genesis 38:14–26?

Read Matthew 1:5. Who is the woman mentioned?

What is one thing we learn about her in Joshua 2:1?

Read Matthew 1:5. Who is the woman mentioned?

What is one thing we learn about her in Ruth 1:1–5?

Matthew 1:6: Who is the woman mentioned?

What is one thing we learn about her 2 Samuel 11:1–5?

There's something we should take notice of—something bold, even audacious, tucked into the genealogy of Jesus. Matthew doesn't just include women, which in itself was rare for Jewish genealogies; he names women from *outside* the Jewish covenant.[10]

Tamar, a Canaanite; Rahab, another Canaanite; Ruth, a Moabite from a nation historically hostile to Israel; and Bathsheba, the wife of Uriah the Hittite. Each of their stories (along with many others in this genealogy) is entangled with brokenness and marked by circumstances that, to human eyes, seem too messy, too complicated for God's plan.

How does the inclusion of diverse backgrounds, nations, and life circumstances communicate a broader message about God's welcome and the future spread of the gospel to all people?

WEEK FIVE: IMPARTIAL CHRIST   143

These women (and men) are not hidden footnotes like some during this day might have hoped; they're central to His-story. Interesting, right? But not nearly as surprising when we trace the patterns we've been following through Scripture all along.

Circle Yes or No. Do you think the inclusion of these women in Jesus' genealogy prepared the way for Mary's extraordinary and unconventional role in Jesus' conception (Matt. 1:18)? Why or why not?

If a new Christian were to ask you: How does God's inclusion of the unexpected demonstrate His power to work through even the most unimaginable family circumstances to accomplish His plan? In two to three sentences, write what you might say.

Jesus didn't come with a flawless "resume." Perfection never needed one. He didn't come to earn redemption. He came to give it, to be the Redeemer who writes broken stories into His perfect plan.

Read Matthew 1:1 again. Think back to what we learned in Week Two about covenants. Why do you think Matthew refers to Jesus as the "Son of Abraham" and the "Son of David" (see Gen. 17:1–8; Jer. 23:5)? How do these titles show Jesus as the fulfillment of God's covenant promises (see 2 Sam. 7:16)?

In one word, how would you describe what this genealogy reveals about the character of God?

How does understanding that Jesus came to bridge the gap between a holy God and broken humanity motivate you to bring the areas of your life that feel irreconcilable to Him? Check any areas you're experiencing.

☐ **Broken relationships:** There are relationships in my life that feel beyond repair, strained connections with a family member, friend, or spouse.

☐ **Emotional struggles:** I'm carrying the weight of bitterness, unforgiveness, and anger.

☐ **Spiritual doubts:** My faith feels like it's slipping away. I wrestle with doubts, and my heart feels distant from God.

☐ **Unmet goals or regrets:** A constant sense of disappointment looms over me in what feels like missed opportunities, past mistakes, and unresolved regrets.

☐ **Health challenges or life circumstances:** Chronic illness, financial struggles, and personal loss all feel overwhelming.

One more thing before we close in response. Look up Matthew 28:1–5. Who does Jesus choose as the very first to carry the good news of His resurrection to the disciples?

Women—grieving, trembling, faithful women. In the first-century Jewish world, a woman's testimony held little to no weight. In most cases, it wasn't even considered valid or reliable in legal or public settings.[11]

Included at the center of God's plan are the unexpected, the overlooked, the ones society deems unqualified. God's kingdom exalts the lowly, enlists the humble, and sends the least likely to declare the greatest news the world has ever heard.

RESPOND:

This genealogy is an invitation, reminding us that God offers another chance to come and be *forever welcomed*.

Reflect on the men and women included in Jesus' genealogy. If Jesus were here in the flesh today, describe who you imagine He would walk alongside.

Are these the same people you feel comfortable welcoming into your life? If not, what is one practical step you could take to start making space to simply notice another?

As we close today, let's ask God to help us . . . *Lord, thank You for the embodiment of Jesus Christ, who generously shows hospitality to sinners. Search my heart, Lord, and reveal the areas where I resist loving as You love. Help me to include the unlikely, notice the overlooked, and reach out to those to whom I find it most difficult to extend Your grace and impartial love. In Jesus' name, amen.*

WEEK FIVE | DAY THREE

Independent of Culture

Before you begin, ask God to open your eyes to His impartial love, that you may read it, receive it, and respond faithfully.

FROM THE TABERNACLE TO THE TABLE

In Week Three, we walked through the tabernacle, which stood as a kind of prophetic glimpse of God's redemptive plan that would one day be fulfilled in Jesus Christ. This portable sanctuary was God teaching Israel—and us—that He desires to dwell among His people, to mold them into a holy, set-apart community that reflects His character to the world.

Everything in it, from the design to the rituals, pointed to Jesus, who is the true fulfillment of God dwelling with us.

In John 1:14, it reads, "The Word became flesh and made his dwelling among us."

John is drawing a straight line back to the rich imagery of the tabernacle. When he says the Word "made his dwelling" among us, it literally means God "tabernacled" among His people.[12] It's like the text is nudging us to remember Exodus.

The God who dwelled in the tabernacle stepped into skin (John 1:14).

As we've been learning throughout this study, the God of the Bible is nothing like the gods worshiped by the distant nations that were empty and distant. This

148   FOREVER WELCOMED

God of the Bible chose to draw near. He chose to step into humanity's dust, walk among us and dwell with us to welcome us.

READ:
John 1:14, Hebrews 9:11, Revelation 21:3

RECEIVE:
There are several correlations between the Old Testament tabernacle where God's presence dwelled and the One who came to dwell with us in the New Testament. Let's take a closer look at some of them.

The table of showbread held the bread of the presence (Ex. 25:30), a reminder that God is the provider, faithfully meeting the needs of His people. What connection do you see between the bread of the presence and what Jesus said in John 6:35?

Jesus is _____.

In the tabernacle, the golden lampstand's warm glow lit up the holy place, reminding us that God's guidance never flickers and His presence never falters. Read John 8:12. What connection do you see between the golden lampstand and Jesus' statement?

Jesus is the _____.

The bronze altar was where sacrifices were made to forgive sin, a reminder of the cost of forgiveness and the need for a substitute. What connection do you see between the sacrifices at the bronze altar and Jesus' statement in John 10:11?

Jesus is the perfect _____.

The entrance to the tabernacle communicated that God's people were invited to draw near in worship to Him. What connection do you see between the tabernacle entrance and Jesus' statement in John 10:9?

Jesus is _____.

WEEK FIVE: IMPARTIAL CHRIST   149

Priests used the tabernacle's bronze basin for ceremonial washing, an act of purification and preparation for serving God. What connection do you see between the purpose of the bronze basin, used for ceremonial purification, and the description of Jesus' work in Ephesians 5:25–26?

> Jesus is the one who _____.

The altar of incense was where the priests burned fragrant incense; the sweet-smelling aroma represented the prayers of God's people rising up to Him. What connection do you see between the priest's intercession at the altar of incense and what Hebrews 7:25 tells us?

> Jesus is the _____.

The veil separated the Holy Place from the Most Holy Place. This thick fabric was a reminder of the barrier that existed between God and humanity. It was only the high priest who could enter, and only once a year. Read Hebrews 10:19–20; what connection do you see between the veil and Jesus' flesh?

> Jesus flesh represents the torn _____ (Heb. 10:19–20).

The ark of the covenant was a sacred, gold-covered chest that held God's covenants. It symbolized God's presence among His people and His covenantal relationship. What connections do you see between the ark of the covenant and Jesus, who is called Immanuel (Matt. 1:23)?

> Jesus is God _____.

Now through Jesus Christ, God has made His followers a temple people (1 Cor. 3:16). God's presence isn't confined to a tent, a temple, or a temporary body anymore. It is moving, active, and alive in us. The same divine presence that once filled the tabernacle—the presence that dwelled fully in Jesus—now lives by His Spirit within every believer. We are not distant observers of God's glory; we are living, breathing sanctuaries of His presence.

But with that indwelling comes a calling. We're set apart to carry His light into a partial world that desperately needs it. Just like the Israelites were called to live differently from the nations surrounding them, we too are called to live in but not of our current cultures.

Read Matthew 5:14–16. In ancient Israel, light was essential for survival, especially after sunset. Write the number of times you notice the word "you," the second-person pronoun, in these verses.

The word "you" in this verse is plural in the original Greek, meaning that Jesus was addressing His disciples as a collective group rather than as individuals. That's important!

What danger can arise when we read passages like these with an individualistic lens?

Jesus here is reminding them—and us—that they are to be His light-bearers *together*. *Together*, they are to live set-apart lives, reflecting His impartial love as a unified temple people. In this way, God's people *light* the way through the darkness to the glorious Light of His kingdom (John 8:12).

RESPOND:
If the enemy were taking a close inventory of your life, what weaknesses, fears, or insecurities might be used to keep you from living set apart? What would distract you from fully being God's light with others (Rom. 12:2)?

Take a moment to underline distractions that might be keeping you from fuller faithfulness:

- ☐ **Social media** — I find myself constantly focused on seeking emotional validation through likes, comments, or followers, making it hard to prioritize God's approval.

- ☐ **Discontentment** — Feelings of inadequacy or comparison with others sometimes prevent me from stewarding my gifts well for the kingdom of God.

- ☐ **Fear of rejection** — I hesitate to share my faith or speak truth to others because I'm afraid of being canceled, misunderstood, or even losing relational opportunities.

- ☐ **Obsession with worldly wins** — I'm at times addicted to pursuing personal goals, acquiring wealth, or maintaining comfort, which leads me to neglect God's peace and eternal priorities.

- ☐ **Busyness** — My life is usually overcrowded with tasks, obligations, and overcommitting, which makes it challenging to create space for God's presence and to share His hospitality with others.

It's never been about what you or I can bring to the table; it's always about what Jesus has already offered us and welcomes us into.

When the distractions of our hearts led us to wander in darkness, let us turn back toward the Light. Jesus' words spoken to His followers in John 8:12 is still true today: "I am the light of the world. Whoever follows me will never walk in darkness, but will have the light of life."

How will you choose to walk in this light today?

WEEK FIVE | DAY FOUR

Identity Reimagined

Before you begin, ask God to open your eyes to His impartial love, that you may read it, receive it, and respond faithfully.

READ:
Matthew 13:34–35

RECEIVE:
Fully God and fully man, Jesus Christ came to dwell in the world, inviting humanity into a new identity and not through any merit or personal achievement of their own. With each encounter, Jesus overturned the world's expectations, showing humanity what it means to be radically welcomed and impartially loved.

Through His parables and His life, Jesus repeatedly defied societal norms. Lean in close, and you'll see how His teachings reveal the surprising reality of who God welcomes.

Look up the word "parable" in the Background Materials on page 206. Then, in your own words, briefly summarize its meaning below.

WEEK FIVE: IMPARTIAL CHRIST

Now, let's debunk a common myth: These parables are not, first and foremost, about you; they are about Jesus and the kingdom He is inaugurating.

You may have grown up hearing something to the effect that parables are "earthly stories with heavenly meanings," but they are so much more.[13] Jesus used parables to invite people into a whole new way of thinking—a kingdom reality that turned expectations upside down.[14]

But to truly grasp the depth of Jesus' parables, we must linger in the teachings, questions, and surrounding context that frame each story.[15]

First, here are three quick things we need to know about the parables:

1. Jewish parables were like an invitation; they drew listeners to discover deep truths that would ultimately bring them to a moment of decision.[16]

2. Jewish teachers often used parables that drew from the ordinary rhythms of daily life—seeds sown in fields, coins exchanged in markets, and the dynamics of the family home.[17]

3. Jewish parables rarely, if ever, included women, and certainly not as main characters. Women in that culture were given little to no opportunities for learning in comparison to men (we'll see more of this later),[18] so modern-day rabbis crafted stories that reflected the experiences of the men who gathered to hear them.

What's one way you think Jesus' parables might differ from those of other rabbis? (Don't worry if you're not yet familiar with Jesus' parables. Just give it your best shot.)

Jesus' parables were revolutionary! They didn't completely follow tradition. Jesus took the familiar and flipped it upside down. *Jesus' parables didn't reinforce the status quo—they redefined it.*

Let's review and complete the chart below. Notice the cultural context of Jesus' parables and how they boldly challenged societal norms. Write how Jesus' view of people differed from societal norms.

Luke 10:25–37 (The Parable of the Good Samaritan)	**Cultural Context:** Samaritans were despised by Jewish people and were considered to be religiously impure and ethnically inferior. A Samaritan helping a Jew would have been shocking and offensive to Jesus' audience. **What Jesus taught:**
Luke 14:15–24 (The Parable of the Great Banquet)	**Cultural Context:** Banquets in Jesus' time were exclusive affairs for the wealthy, powerful, and socially esteemed. Honor and status were everything in this culture, and the guest list reflected a person's place in society. **What Jesus taught:**

WEEK FIVE: IMPARTIAL CHRIST

Luke 15:11–32 (The Parable of the Prodigal Son)	**Cultural Context:** In this culture, the younger son was not typically entitled to the primary inheritance or the honor of carrying on the family legacy, which was a privilege that belonged to the elder son. For a younger son to demand his inheritance while the father was still alive was an insult, similar to wishing his father dead.[19] Squandering that inheritance in a foreign land only worsens the disgrace, staining the family's name and standing in the community. **What Jesus taught:**
Luke 18:1–8 (The Parable of the Persistent Widow and the Unjust Judge)	**Cultural Context:** Widows were among the most vulnerable members of society, often left powerless and without resources to demand justice—especially when facing corrupt officials who prioritized the wealthy and influential. **What Jesus taught:**

True or False: Through His teachings, Jesus Christ offers a reimagined identity, extending it even to those society considers unworthy or unwelcomed.

Choose two parables from the chart above that spoke to you personally or stirred something within your heart. Why do these examples stand out to you?

Reflecting back on what we learned about the prophets in Week Four, do you see any connections between Jesus' teachings and the messages of the prophets? Write at least one observation. Hint: Consider the people the prophets warned not to overlook (Zech. 7:9–10).

TUGGING THE THREADS: At the time of Jesus' earthly ministry, it's likely that Jewish men recited daily prayers called the *Birkot Hashachar*, which had been passed down orally but were later recorded in the Jewish Talmud.[20] The Talmud consists of recorded teachings and debates of Jewish law and tradition. It is still used to this day around the world in Jewish schools. In the morning's blessings, Jewish men expressed gratitude to God for not being born into a socially disadvantaged status of a Gentile, a slave, or a woman.[21]

Put yourself in the shoes of a foreigner, slave, or woman in that culture for a moment. Consider what it was like to live on the edge of society. To know, that no matter how much you wanted to belong, you would always be kept at a distance, always reminded of your place on the fringes.

WEEK FIVE: IMPARTIAL CHRIST   157

> And then, one day, you hear Jesus, the long-awaited Messiah, tell a parable, because He invited you, a woman, to listen and learn. And in this one parable, a person with your status is a central figure.

Don't miss this: Radical hospitality beats at the very heart of the gospel, inviting us to see both ourselves and others through the lens of God's impartial love.

Jesus didn't just tell stories about inviting people in. He lived the message too.

Below, draw a line matching the story on the left to the people involved in that specific encounter with Jesus on the right. Consider how Jesus' life reflected His teachings as He connected with real people.

Jesus dignifies a woman caught in sin, restoring her sense of value and social standing far beyond her past actions.	Mark 16:1–8
Jesus entrusted women as the first witnesses to His resurrection, in a society where a woman's testimony was not considered valid in a court of law.	John 8:1–11
Jesus invited women to learn in a culture where women were not invited to be disciples of a rabbi.	Luke 10:38–42

RESPOND:

These stories remind us that God's love, mercy, and grace are for all who come and receive His welcome, His way. How is He calling you to respond and live out the reimagined identity He offers today?

- Taking a prayer walk, inviting God to speak into a situation.

- Making that phone call to reconcile a situation that's been weighing on your heart.

- Humbly apologizing for the way you treated someone.

- Intentionally welcoming someone into your home this week with the hospitable love of Jesus.

- Letting go of the ways you compare yourself to others—their opportunities, their parenting styles, their physical looks—and resting in the truth of who God has created *you* to be.

- Showing impartial love to your spouse, paying attention to rather than overlooking their needs.

We welcome others because God has so generously welcomed us.

WEEK FIVE | DAY FIVE

Impartial Love

Before you begin, ask God to open your eyes to His impartial love, that you may read it, receive it, and respond faithfully.

Christ came to earth, embodying God's impartiality toward sinners in need of saving, and that changes everything. But His plan of redemption was not Plan B. This rescue was in play from the beginning. Let's spend a little time today looking at how the ways Christ came to us foreshadowed the lengths to which He'd go to save us.

READ:
Luke 2:4–7, Matthew 27:57–61

RECEIVE:

There were many ways in which Jesus' birth foretold of His resurrection. Match the details about His birth on the left with the details about His death and resurrection on the right.[22]

Jesus experienced rejection at His birth (Mark 6:4; Matt. 2:16).

Jesus was wrapped in swaddling cloths shortly after His birth (Luke 2:7).

Jesus was born in a manger, a stone structure (Luke 2:7).

Angels announced Jesus' birth to the shepherds, proclaiming the good news of His arrival (Luke 2:10–11).

Jesus was laid in a tomb after His crucifixion, a man-made stone structure (Matt. 27:57–60).

After Jesus' resurrection, angels were the first to announce that Jesus was alive, speaking to the women who came to His tomb (Matt. 28:5–7).

Jesus' death was marked by rejection. He was crucified outside the city on a hill called Golgotha, and despised by many (John 19:17–18).

At His death, Jesus was wrapped in linen cloths by Joseph of Arimathea and laid in a tomb (Mark 15:46).

Take a moment to skim back over the list. Where do you see God's radical welcome in both Jesus' birth and resurrection (hint, take note of who was present)?

WEEK FIVE: IMPARTIAL CHRIST   161

List two ways this encourages you to trust God's promises that are yet to come, even as you see and experience the brokenness of our world.

From His humble entry in a stone manger
to His resurrection from a stone tomb,
these are the bookends of a story in which death is undone.
And with His last breath, He breathed life into humanity.

As you reflect on this week, where have you seen God's impartial love in surprising ways?

We don't want to miss God's impartial love breaking into our lives just because it doesn't fit into what we imagine or because we assume it's meant for *"that person over there."* God's love can't be contained by our expectations. He loves with infinite capacity, showing up in the places and people we might easily overlook. God's love moves where, how, and through whom He chooses.

Was there a thread from this week—Made in His Image, Included in God's Plan, Independent of Culture, or Identity Reimagined that stood out to you the most? How did it connect to your personal story?

In what truths is God inviting you to trust more deeply? Check all that apply.

- ☐ God's love for me is not diminished by my recent failures.

- ☐ God's love for me stays constant, even in this prolonged season of loneliness.

- ☐ God's love for me remains steady as I work to break down walls of self-sufficiency.

- ☐ God's love for me doesn't waver; it welcomes me in, even when others reject or misunderstand me.

- ☐ God's love never grows distant in my season of grief.

- ☐ God's love reaches down into the most unlikely spaces, places we might never dare to look.

RESPOND:

When God's people needed a second chance, He provided it through Jesus Christ—the new Adam, the One who restored what was broken and offered life where death once reigned.

WEEK FIVE: IMPARTIAL CHRIST   163

How does reading about Jesus' power over the grave encourage you to bring Him the areas in which you're experiencing a form of death or hopelessness?

If God chooses not to resurrect areas of our lives in this season, may it not be because we didn't ask. We can trust in His will as we wait for the full resurrection that is to come.

WEEK SIX | IMPARTIAL CHURCH

Impartial Church

Jesus promised that no force of darkness, no scheme of division or discord, could ever prevail against the church built on Him as its solid foundation. From the Gospels to the Epistles, the consistent theme is that the church is called to mirror God's pattern of radical, impartial love. In Christ, the doors are flung wide open with an invitation, and all who come and receive Him are forever welcome, knitted into His family with grace.

The Price of Belonging

Picture walking the streets of a first-century Roman city, where invisible structures govern every part of your daily life—the systems known as patronage and brokerage.[1] Your ability to improve your circumstances depends in part on your relationship with someone of higher status: a patron— a person of influence. This patron provides financial support, protection, employment opportunities, and even advocacy in legal matters to their client.[2]

Their status is your security, and their power is a source of borrowed worth in this society.

As a client in Roman society, likely from the lower class, you are at the mercy of someone else's influence and power. Some mornings, you'd find yourself rising before dawn, making your way to their house, and waiting—sometimes for hours—just to be addressed with a need for work or dismissed without a word.[3] In exchange for a patron's favor, you would owe loyalty, service, and public praise. And though there was a transactional nature of the relationship, proximity to the power of a patron meant security and a sense of belonging.

The role of brokerage was another role in everyday life. A broker acted as a go-between, interceding and advocating to connect clients with patrons.

And here's where it gets interesting. This mindset of transactions and influence seeped into the spaces of religious interactions as well. Just as political patrons wielded power through wealth and influence, religious "patrons" held a different kind of currency, one that was spiritual. Some leaders positioned themselves as the gatekeepers of God's favor, offering access to blessings, guidance, and a sense of belonging in exchange for idolatrous devotion and loyalty.

In whatever realm of society you found yourself, the same underlying reality remained—*Who you knew often mattered more than who you were.*

Understanding this cultural backdrop gives us insight into why favoritism and partiality were challenges in the early church. Social hierarchies dominated these societies where power and privilege were not shared equally. The early church wrestled with what it meant to live in a community where God's grace, not social standing, defined one's place.

But first, I want to ask you: Do you believe these same pressures and temptations exist in the church today?

In this chapter, we'll enter into the story of the early church and observe how they, like us, were called to live by a different standard: one that sees people through the lens of God's impartial love.

In God's kingdom, we are not welcomed because of status, wealth, or influence but on the basis of His abundant grace.

WEEK SIX | DAY ONE

Made in God's Image

Before you begin, ask God to open your eyes to His impartial love, that you may read it, receive it, and respond faithfully.

Context: As we enter this final week of our journey, we arrive in the pages of the New Testament, where both the penetrating and practical words of the writer James, along with other biblical passages, speak directly to God's often overlooked attribute of impartiality.

Who, exactly, is James?

James was the half-brother of Jesus and also a pillar of the early church. He was a steadfast leader in Jerusalem whose influence helped shape the Christian faith in its earliest and most fragile days.[4] His voice lent wisdom and stability as the gospel spread in a world that was often hostile to its message (Gal. 2:9, 12).

For more than twenty years, James poured his very life into the growing church. It was rumored that James prayed so often that he had calloused knees like that of a camel. Day by day, James remained committed to shepherding believers through seasons of intense persecution and hardship, including the devastating famines that they experienced.[5] Ultimately, his dedication led him to martyrdom. Yet even now, the words he has written are as fresh to us now as they were then, continuing to call God's people to an impartial faith that endures.

READ:

James 2:1–5

RECEIVE:

Looking at James 2:1 written out for you below, mark the word partiality with a small cross.

> "My brothers [or brothers and sisters], show no partiality as you hold the faith in our Lord Jesus Christ, the Lord of glory" (James 2:1 ESV).

What imagery does James use to show that favoritism contradicts faith in Jesus? Write your thoughts or express them through a drawing that captures his message.

How does the practice of holding on to both the faith and to partiality fall short of reflecting the image and character of God?

TUGGING THE THREADS: In James 2:1, the word partiality links to the Greek term *prosōpolēmpsia*, which derives from Old Testament imagery. The equivalent Hebrew (the primary language used in the Old Testament) phrase often translates this expression as "receiving the face of" (*nāśā' pānīm*).[6] It depicts a ruler or judge "lifting the face" of someone they favor or "casting it down" when they disapprove.[7] It's a way of illustrating favoritism, where someone's worth is determined by external factors such as status, wealth, or physical appearance. James is saying that when we show partiality, we put ourselves in the place of judging someone's worth!

Look up the following verses and write each in the space below:

Leviticus 19:15:

Deuteronomy 10:17:

What do both of these verses show us about God's character as it's displayed in the Old Testament?

James's Jewish-Christian audience would have been familiar with these Old Testament books. In chapter 1, James calls his readers "the twelve tribes scattered . . ." scattered—like seeds flung far from home. James is writing to Jewish believers, dispersed by the fierce winds of persecution, torn from their homes, their communities, and in some cases even their families.[8]

WEEK SIX: IMPARTIAL CHURCH   171

In the first century, society was sharply divided into two economic classes: the fabulously wealthy and the struggling poor. The wealthy made up only about 2 percent of the population. While most Christians did not belong to this elite group, some did. James's audience included a mix—some wealthy, though a small minority, others poor and oppressed, and still a few others holding positions of influence yet facing persecution for their faith (James 1:9–11, 27; 5:1–6).[9]

Review James 2:1–5, keeping the context in mind. What might have made favoritism feel normal or more acceptable, even though it went against the heart of God?

Can you personally relate to any of these reasons that made partiality feel normal? How?

The social climate in which James wrote was one where influence belonged to the few. Many of his readers lived in a society stacked against them. They felt the weight of injustice pressing down and the sting of marginalization because of their faith. They may have felt unseen and unheard, yet they were never forgotten by the impartial God who sees and knows all.

Look closely at James 2:1. What familial greeting does he use to address those he's writing to?

172   FOREVER WELCOMED

Even as James prepares to correct his brothers and sisters, how does this identification, even in rebuke, show his recognition of their inherent value as image bearers?

In what way do you see James model the very message he's about to deliver in James 2?

Their world revolved around the rhythm of *we* instead of simply *me*, a culture where the strength of the whole was prioritized over personal achievement.[10] In this communal way of living, the driving question wasn't, "How does this apply to *me*?" but rather, "How does this shape *us*?"

As we read James's words this week, try to make note of the distinctive difference between their worldview and ours. In our Western culture, we gravitate toward independence and self-reliance, and thus, we can unintentionally limit our understanding of Scripture by approaching it with a hyper-individualistic view. But the gospel calls us to see beyond personal application to a vision of *shared* transformation.

What would it change if we asked, "How can we, as the body of Christ, actively work together against showing partiality, not just as individuals, but as a community?"

WEEK SIX: IMPARTIAL CHURCH

Consider your current community or church group. What do you think it would look like to pursue reflecting the image of God collectively, not just individually? What are some areas you need to grow in? (Examples could include joining a group at church, mentoring someone, or finding a mentor to grow in faith.)

As we step into this week and lean into the call to be an *Impartial Church*, let's ask the Lord to widen our perspective and open our hearts, not just individually but communally so that we may reflect His image together.

Take a moment to notice the title James uses for Jesus in verse 1. It's unique and packed with meaning. If you're able, say it aloud: *Our Lord Jesus Christ, the Lord of glory* (James 2:1 ESV).

The title, *the Lord of glory*, is only used twice in the entire New Testament (see also 1 Cor. 2:8). So, why do you think James chose this specific title here, out of all Jesus' other titles as he exhorts his brothers and sisters to reject partiality?

When we show partiality, who are we really giving glory to? In what way?

RESPOND:

It wouldn't take much for James's words to pierce right through our very living rooms, boardrooms, and sanctuaries. Can we be honest? What the writer James describes feels like it holds up a mirror not just toward our own culture but even to our own hearts. He describes a faith being professed with lips while favoritism and partiality take root deep in hearts.

This age-old tendency to seize the glory that belongs to God alone and lay it at the feet of mere humans (including ourselves) persists today. Yes, humans are crowned with a type of glory, but we are not to take that which belongs to God alone— His worship and reverence. That weight of glory is His alone to hold.

But, when the church reflects His heart, the world sees His glory.

How is God inviting you to respond to His glory today? (Look up "glory" in the Background Materials on page 204 for guidance.)

WEEK SIX | DAY TWO

Included in God's Plan

Before you begin, ask God to open your eyes to His impartial love, that you may read it, receive it, and respond faithfully.

READ:

James 2:3–4

RECEIVE:

Look up James 2:3–4 in the different translations below. Pay close attention to how each one offers a unique insight into these verses . . .

ESV: And if you _____ to the one who wears the fine clothing.

NIV: And if you _____ to the one who wears the fine clothing.

CSB: And if you _____ to the one who wears the fine clothing.

Which reading stands out to you the most and why?

How do the different phrases in each translation shed light on the subtle (and not so subtle) ways partiality can manifest itself?

Look again at James 2:2–3. Based on the cultural context we noted on Day 1, how might the person's fine clothing have been seen by others as a sign of God's blessing or a means of provision during their trials?

Based on James 2:2–3. How do you think our self-perception influences the way we treat the people around us?

Do you think that showing favoritism sometimes reveals more about our own hearts—our insecurities, desires, and unfulfilled "needs"—than it does about the other person?

Have you ever felt like you're standing on the outside, watching others step into the blessings and favor that you've been praying for? Have you ever wondered if they're somehow more chosen, more *included in God's plans* than you? Highlight any of the following circumstances that resonate with you:

- Someone else recently received an opportunity I had been working hard toward.

- I recently watched a close friend get married. I celebrated her deeply, but part of me couldn't ignore the ache that I'm still single.

- I just heard of another pregnancy, and if I'm honest, it stung. That's the miracle I've been praying for, and it still hasn't come.

- I've been noticing a peer's influence rise while it feels like my voice is losing relevance.

- It's hard seeing my friend's kids excel in school while I'm praying my child makes it through another week without struggle or tears.

- While a coworker climbs the ladder, I feel like I'm standing still.

- This wife is sharing stories of spiritual breakthroughs, and I'm over here just trying to find five quiet minutes with God.

Deep down, have you ever thought or felt that God was being flat-out partial—showing favor to others in ways that felt unfair? Write down what emotions you experienced; God can handle your honesty.

What is one truth from our study of God's Word so far that can help encourage you in these moments?

It's also helpful for us to remember here God's common grace, which flows out of His impartial love (Matt. 5:45). As James points out in the first chapter of his letter, "Every good and perfect gift is from above, coming down from the Father of the heavenly lights, who does not change like shifting shadows" (James 1:17). God gives general blessings and can choose to restrain evil regardless of one's faith or lack of faith in Him. And we can praise Him for that, even when we aren't the recipients at that moment.

How we understand God's favor also frames how we see who's included in His plan—*including ourselves.* Sometimes, we may overlook the quiet, faithful ways He's already at work in our lives.

Read James 2:2, and then take a moment to look up "gold rings" in the Background Materials on page 207 to understand their significance in this culture. Explain below what gold rings are in one sentence.

For a minute, picture the scene in your mind that James so vividly describes in James 2:4–5. Do you see the "gold rings" and "shining garments"—those visible symbols of worth and success that dazzle our eyes and capture our attention? They make us pause and, if we're honest, sometimes even bow in subtle reverence.

Write down what you believe to be the markers of prestige in the society we live in today.

WEEK SIX: IMPARTIAL CHURCH   179

Fill in the blank below with examples James might call out if he were speaking to us in our culture today. (There is no wrong answer, but I've provided an example: *If a man or woman having a large social media platform walks into your assembly and a woman with no popular social standing also comes in.)*

If a man or woman _____

_____.

Is it wrong for a believer to have or desire outward wealth, like "gold rings" or "fine clothing"? Why or why not?

Don't miss this small detail. Read James 2:3–4. Who is James rebuking in this verse? Circle your answer.

    a) the poor man

    b) the wealthy man

    c) the one who shows partiality, judging between the rich and the poor

Look up Romans 16:1–2. At the end of verse 2, it says that Phoebe "has been a _____ of many . . ."

Paul describes her as a benefactor or *patroness*, one who used her wealth, resources, and influence to help God's people. Although Scripture doesn't give us every detail, it's clear Phoebe offered substantial support to the early church in many ways.[11] What we do know is that her service left a significant impact on the community, including Paul himself, so much so that he takes the time to commend her publicly.

In the church, we don't climb over each other to get ahead. We bend low to serve one another.

Consider other examples from Scripture, including Joseph of Arimathea who used his wealth to provide a tomb for Jesus (Matt. 27:57–59), Lydia who sold purple cloth and was known for her business and generosity (Acts 16:14), and the Ethiopian eunuch who was a high-ranking official with great resources (Acts 8:27). Scripture warns us about a sinful love of money (1 Tim. 6:1), but it also urges us to steward well what we've been entrusted with (Matt. 25:14–30).

How does Phoebe's story, along with the other examples, show us how to steward influence and wealth in a way that serves God's kingdom? Instead of only using our positions to climb higher, how can we choose to lift others up?

RESPOND:
Where in your life do you find yourself measuring what God has placed in your hands against what He's laid on the palms of others? What are those quiet moments when the ache of not enough creeps in and whispers that you're missing out?

Comparison has a way of distorting our vision, leading us to perceive God's goodness as partial, limited, or unwisely distributed. Can I encourage you to allow the truth of God's Word to gently dismantle those lies, reminding you that His plans for you are always good? Here are a few truths to hold on to . . .

We are God's workmanship, created for specific good works He prepared for us to do (Eph. 2:10).

God has written our story, and His timing is perfect (Ps. 139:16).

God has placed us in the body of Christ exactly as He intended (1 Cor. 12:18).

We can celebrate the gifts and blessings of others, knowing we are all part of one body, united in the same mission (1 Cor. 12:27).

Included in God's plan, eternally welcomed: that's who *you* are, child of God.

WEEK SIX | DAY THREE

Independent of Culture

Before you begin, ask God to open your eyes to His impartial love, that you may read it, receive it, and respond faithfully.

READ:
James 2:3–5, Matthew 5:3–12

RECEIVE:
Look up "meritocracy" in the Background Materials on page 206. In your own words, briefly summarize what it is.

Do you believe a culture of meritocracy has crept into the church today? Why or why not?

> **TUGGING THE THREADS:** Seating arrangements in the first-century era meant something. In places where people gathered to worship and learn, like the synagogue, your seating placement indicated your status and influence within the community (Luke 11:43; 14:7–31).

Read Matthew 23:1–6. Which group of people did Jesus say loved the high seats and places of honor?

They carry the rulebook in their hands,
but the pages never seep into their hearts.

What's the irony in those who position themselves as religious leaders and keepers of the law, yet fail to actually follow God's commands? Check all that apply.

☐ They were called to guard God's law in truth, but instead, they twisted it to serve their own partiality (Matt. 23:16).

☐ They imposed heavy burdens that reflected influence of the culture rather than God's command (Matt. 23:4).

☐ Their actions completely contradicted the impartial and just nature of the God they claimed to represent (Matt. 23:23).

Look up James 3:1. What grave warning does this offer to you and me today? Are we safe from falling into the same trap just because we know God's Word?

The teachings of James mirror Jesus' words and closely reflect the Beatitudes found in Matthew 5:3–12. If you haven't already, please read Matthew 5:3–12.

Both Jesus and James advocate a revolutionary way of life that runs *independently of culture's* values.

In the Beatitudes, Jesus presents a counter-cultural definition of what it means to be truly blessed. And here's something really important to keep in mind—Jesus' teachings in the Beatitudes are indicative, not imperative. Jesus is not handing out a to-do list of commands to follow, but rather He's making a statement about reality.[12] He's saying *if* you find yourself in these states—whether in mourning, humility, or spiritual hunger—you are blessed, even if your culture says otherwise.

Jesus is not ignoring the pain that comes with these experiences, and He's certainly not advertising suffering for suffering's sake. What He *is* doing is making a radical claim:

that these difficult places in life can actually become the very spaces where we encounter God's presence and grace in a transformative way.

In the chart below, take a moment to reflect on how each Beatitude outlines the kingdom's way of life. In the right column, write down words or phrases that represent the world's ideals next to each Beatitude. I have done the first two as examples.

Kingdom Values	Culture Claims
Example: Blessed are the poor	*Blessed are the prideful, self-sufficient, and independent*
Example: Blessed are those who mourn	*Blessed are those who pursue the avoidance of pain and the pleasure of happiness at all cost*
Blessed are the meek	Blessed are the _____ _____ _____

Blessed are the merciful	Blessed are the _____
Blessed are the peacemakers	Blessed are the _____
Blessed are those who hunger and thirst for righteousness	Blessed are the _____

In the Beatitudes, it's almost as if Jesus is saying, "*You're looking for blessing in all the wrong places. You've been taught to chase after power, success, and recognition. But true blessing—the kind that lasts—is found in the places you least expect and often think you want to avoid at all costs.*"

What societal measures are you sometimes tempted to use when deciding who is and who is not blessed? Do these filters line up or clash with the kind of blessing Jesus describes in the Beatitudes?

It's easy, isn't it, to begin to accept the world's definitions of "lack" and "abundance"? I see it in my own life. But what if the situation we see as "lack" is leading us to depend on God's provision (and not our own)? What if what we perceive as lack is actually positioning us to receive God's true abundance?

RESPOND:

The Beatitudes invite us into a deeper understanding of who God truly is, One who steps into our very struggles *with* us (Heb. 4:15). Though we know deep down that God meets us in our pain and our joy, we often just *forget*. That's why, throughout Scripture, God calls over and over again to remember. Not because He forgets but because He knows how easily we do.

This simple act of remembering stirs our hearts with fresh expectancy that the God who has been faithful before will surely be faithful again.

Take one final look at those Beatitudes (Matt. 5:3–12). Where have you seen God at work in your life or in the lives of those around you? Has He met you in your grief and comforted you (Matt. 5:4)? Has He filled you when you've hungered and thirsted for righteousness (Matt. 5:6)? Or perhaps He's given you supernatural strength to be a peacemaker in a difficult situation (Matt. 5:9)? Respond below.

Remember, remember, remember how God has shown up for you. Trace back over the path of His faithfulness, and as you do, you'll likely see not just the moments when He met you but the countless times He's been carrying you through.

Use the line below as a timeline to write three to five ways God has shown up for you or someone you love this year. Create marks on this line and recall under each mark how God has been faithful.

WEEK SIX | DAY FOUR

Identity Reimagined

Before you begin, ask God to open your eyes to His impartial love, that you may read it, receive it, and respond faithfully.

READ:
James 2:1–5

RECEIVE:
Observe James 2:4 written below in the Christian Standard Bible (CSB) version. Circle the word *distinctions* and underline the phrase *judges with evil thoughts* in the passage below.

> "Haven't you made distinctions among yourselves and become judges with evil thoughts?" (James 2:4 CSB)

Look up Proverbs 11:1 and Proverbs 20:10, then fill in the following blanks:

Proverbs 11:1 — "The LORD detests _____ scales, but _____ weights find favor with him."

Proverbs 20:10 — "_____ weights and _____ measures—the LORD detests them both."

188   FOREVER WELCOMED

Do you think the imagery of dishonest and differing weights in Proverbs refers only to literal measurements, or could it also symbolize unfairness in judgment and the treatment of others? Why or why not?

What similarities do you notice between the differing or unequal measures in Proverbs 11:1 and 20:10, and the usage of distinctions described in James 2:3–4?

> **TUGGING THE THREADS:** "Glory" in the Old Testament, *kabod* (בָּכוֹד), means "weight" or "heaviness." This word reflects the expression of God's character.[13] What we give weight, reveals the true *posture* of our hearts (Matt. 6:21).

Look up "church" in the Background Materials on page 205. Why do you think the church is also referred to as the "called out ones"?

I can't help but play out this scene in James 2:3–4. I picture myself walking into that early church gathering, where the smells of freshly baked bread blends with the faint scent of dust from worn sandals. There are murmurs and a buzz of talk throughout the room as people are being assigned their seats.

Those wearing fine clothing are ushered in with warm smiles and eager handshakes. Others shuffle in quietly, heads lowered. Their rugged garments are frayed with thin patches, nearly transparent and falling apart. These individuals are barely noticed, quietly directed to the edges, almost as if they don't belong there at all.

*As my eyes scan the room,
the social divisions are impossible to miss.*

With this scene in mind, consider the *weight* of James's words, tilting the atmosphere with tension and exposing how partiality has led their hearts to be off-kilter:

> If you show special attention to the man wearing fine clothes and say, "Here's a good seat for you," but say to the poor man, "You stand there" or "Sit on the floor by my feet," have you not discriminated among yourselves and become judges with evil thoughts? (James 2:3–4)

Steady your attention on James 2:3. Before we move on, take a stab at this question: When telling the poor man to "sit here by my feet" or "under my footstool," as some Bible translations put it, how are they treating him?

a) As someone who is welcomed and offered an identity reimagined in God's kingdom

b) As someone seen as one whom God opposes (see Ps. 110:1)

Now, let's zoom in on the word "footstool" used in some versions of James 2:3. Look up the Scripture passages in the left column, then write in the right column whether the verse refers to "the Lord's authority" or to "the Lord's enemies."

The Lord's Authority or The Lord's Enemies?

Isaiah 66:1	
1 Kings 5:3	
Mark 12:36	
Luke 20:43	
Hebrews 1:13	

Remember earlier how we discussed that the seat someone occupies can say a lot about their worth in society? In Jesus' time, the honored seats represented those coveted places of privilege, which often came with a footstool.[14] Sitting in that seat with a footstool beneath them was a way of saying "I'm elevated, I am of importance" in the social order.

Take another look at the chart you worked through. What are the two primary ways "footstool" is used in Scripture?

When, whether through our words or our actions, we say to someone, "You sit down at my feet," we are exercising authority that belongs to the Lord, and we are treating them as His _____.

Read James 1:9–10. How does this self-elevating mindset contrast with the reimagined identity God impartially gives to those who come to Him?

It's humbling to pause and reflect on the dual imagery of the footstool in Scripture. In our pride, we can sometimes elevate ourselves above others by reducing them to objects beneath us. The footstool reminds us of both God's sovereign reign over us and the sin that distorts our relationships with others.

James reveals the root issue in James 2:3 (similar to Jesus in Luke 6:45). What does he say they have become? Judges with _____?

The concept of "judging" in this passage carries a tension that's worth unpacking. Judgment can sometimes refer to discernment, a wise and holy evaluation that aligns with God's wisdom and character. But then there's the other kind of judgment: the sinful behavior of elevating some while belittling others, often based on personal bias or superficial appearances.

Which form of distinctions do you think James is referring to in James 2:4? Why?

When we're not sure whether our judgments are right, let's look again to Jesus' example. Instead of seeking the most esteemed seat in the house, Jesus knelt to serve. Instead of stepping on others, He lifted them up. In His kingdom, there are no footstools of superiority. Rather, there is an invitation to sit at the same table, side-by-side, equally and impartially loved.

Read Revelation 5:9, and fill in the blanks:

By His blood, Jesus has purchased for God persons "from every _____ and _____ and _____ and _____."

Read that verse aloud twice—slowly—and do your best to take it in. Just sit with it for a moment and ponder its sheer wonder. Think about the privilege it is that you and I are *welcomed* into this restored kingdom. Not just as distant observers but as active participants.

RESPOND:

What tasks are you most tempted to see as under your feet or "beneath you"? How does considering Christ, who "humbled himself by becoming obedient to death—even death on a cross" (Phil. 2:8), challenge your outlook, even today?

How does God's promise to offer us a *reimagined identity*—spoken long before you or I ever drew a breath (Rev. 5)—encourage you in your spiritual journey?

One more day of walking this journey together.

WEEK SIX: IMPARTIAL CHURCH

WEEK SIX | DAY FIVE

Impartial Love

Before you begin, ask God to open your eyes to His impartial love, that you may read it, receive it, and respond faithfully.

Yesterday, we saw that partiality in the church isn't just a modern-day issue. James tackled it head-on in his letter, and as we'll see today, it's a thread that runs throughout Scripture. The same subtle but strong temptation to elevate influence over integrity, culture over compassion, status over servanthood, and comfort over God's call to love impartially is still very much at work in our human hearts. Yet so is the ever-present, ever-able power of God to overcome it.

READ:

Matthew 16:18

RECEIVE:

Fill in the blank using the verse you just read in Matthew 16:18:

"And I tell you that you are Peter, and on this rock, _____ _____, and the _____ will not overcome it."

194   FOREVER WELCOMED

TUGGING THE THREADS: Jesus calls Peter by name and uses deliberate wordplay. *Peter*, the Greek word *Petros* (Πέτρος) translates to "rock" or "small stone."[15] Jesus uses Peter's name to speak into the heart of God's kingdom plan. Put a pin here; we'll return to it in a moment.

Let's fast-forward a little. Turn to Acts 10:27–35. What does Peter learn about God's character and His view of all people?

Now fast-forward just a little more in the New Testament and read Galatians 2:11–16. What struggle is Peter still dealing with in this passage?

How does Peter's own struggle reveal the tension that exists between faith and practice, especially when societal or cultural pressures challenge what we believe?

The very person who would be instrumental in the building of God's church— the apostle Peter—struggled with partiality, *the very thing that could hinder the furthering of the gospel.*

WEEK SIX: IMPARTIAL CHURCH   195

But God gives more grace. God is at work, even in His followers' struggles and failures, His mission remains unstoppable, and He has promised to build His church—even with imperfect people.

How does reading about Peter's struggle encourage you to be honest about your own, knowing that God extends more grace?

The truth is that even the most faithful followers and leaders in Jesus' church can struggle with partiality. No one is immune to the brokenness that chips away at the world around us.

Any welcome we extend to others is an overflow of the welcome we've already received from God. It's grace upon grace poured out.

Remember when I asked you to put a pin in the name Jesus uses for Peter? Let's come back to it now. In that verse, Jesus says, "And I tell you that you are Peter, and on this rock I will build my church, and the gates of Hades will not overcome it."

In one or two sentences, describe in your own words the promise Jesus makes about the enduring strength of His church.

TUGGING THE THREADS When Jesus speaks these eight words, "the gates of Hades will not overcome it" (Matt. 16:18), He is drawing from both a historical reality and a theological truth. Jesus currently stood in the region of Caesarea Philippi, at the foot of Mount Hermon (Matt. 16:13). At this place existed a cave-like shrine honoring the Greek god Pan. Many people during the time of Jesus believed this to be the entrance to the underworld or Hades—the realm of the dead—a place of utter hunger and thirst.[16]

And here Jesus stands—fully alive, fully present—right in the shadow of that gate, and with complete authority, He declares, "The gates of Hades will not overcome it."

In other words, Jesus is saying that no force of darkness—not even death itself or the powers of evil—can defeat the work of God. His church will endure because its foundation rests upon the One who triumphed over death.

In AD 70, about four decades after Jesus proclaims this promise, the physical second temple in Jerusalem (Ezra 6:14–15) had been destroyed. How do you think Jesus' words in Matthew 16:18 of an enduring church brought hope to some of His followers living in that era?

Read 1 Peter 2:5a. Who is speaking and to what does he compare God's people spiritually? _____ Why do you think this is so significant given the context we've studied today?

WEEK SIX: IMPARTIAL CHURCH   197

Like Peter, a small stone, we too are called into uncomfortable places to be built into something better together than we could be apart.

Before we prepare to close our study in response, let's allow Peter's words, inspired by the Holy Spirit, to encourage us one more time. Later in his life, in his own letters, Peter revisits these themes with wisdom.

Read 1 Peter 1:17, printed below, out loud:

> "Since you call on a Father who judges each person's work impartially,
> live out your time as foreigners here in reverent fear."

Peter now teaches with full assurance about God's character and His eternal welcome. And this knowledge has implications for how we live in reverential *fear here on earth*. Peter's growth reminds us that God is patient with our struggles. As we submit to Him, He reshapes our hearts to align more fully with His impartial love.

Where you started this study is not where you're ending this study. Because there is hope for you too.

RESPOND:

We opened our study by learning about the concept of *shema*, an ancient practice that calls us to move beyond passive listening and into intentional action.

I can tell you, for me personally, moving from knowledge to action isn't always as simple as I'd like it to be. It takes more than just desire or good intentions. It often takes some Holy Spirit–empowered strategy.

As we near the end of our study, I want to return us to the hope expressed in the introduction of this study—our desire to seek to embody God's Word.

Ask yourself, given all the Lord has deposited within me through His Word during this study, what does it look like for me to move toward action? What strategy is God inviting me to implement as I step forward into His eternal welcome?

In the boxes below, write honestly about intentional steps you can take by the power of the Holy Spirit to receive and extend God's welcome. Take as much time as you need to reflect. See the example below for help.

Example:

In the Home:	*Within the next month, I'll invite my neighbor* _____ over for dinner.

In the Home:	
At Work:	
In the Church:	
With Neighbors or Friends:	

Allow this chart to be the start of your intentional strategy. Then, read the following declarations aloud to remind yourself of the incredible welcome God has *already* extended to you.

WEEK SIX: IMPARTIAL CHURCH   199

These declarations weave together the key threads we've explored throughout our journey in the ***Forever Welcomed*** study.

I am God's creation, made in His image and endowed with His glory.
I am included in God's plan, never to be forsaken or abandoned.
I am called and empowered by the Spirit of God to live in but not of the world.
I am given an identity I could never imagine that is shaped by God's Word and His purpose, not by the world's standards.
I am loved impartially, not for what I could ever do but because of what's been done on the cross for me.
I am forever welcomed into His eternal presence, right here and now.
I am forever welcomed by God.

Say it as many times as you need to. Say it when you do and don't believe it. Say it when you're afraid. Say it when you're doubtful and even when you're hopeful. **Because you are welcome too, forever.**

PRAYER OF FAITH

Before we part ways, if you've never placed your faith in Jesus Christ, would you take this moment to do so? In Revelation 3:20, the God of the universe extends the ultimate welcome into life forever . . .

"Here I am! I stand at the door and knock.
If anyone hears my voice and opens the door,
I will come in and eat with that person, and they with me."
(Rev. 3:20)

Jesus came to restore what sin has broken, and today, God offers you one of the most powerful invitations in all of the biblical story: a new heart and renewed purpose in Him. Pray and ask the Lord to forgive your sins, and invite Jesus to take His rightful place in your life as you surrender your heart wholly to Him. You might pray something like this:

Father, I thank You that salvation is found in no other name in heaven or on earth but Jesus Christ (Acts 4:12). It is by His life, death, and resurrection that I can find complete forgiveness and restoration. I acknowledge my sins before you, and I ask that your Holy Spirit would empower me to live in obedience to your commands. I trust in Your wonder-working power to live for Your glory and to walk confidently in the life You offer me daily.

In Jesus' name, amen.

If you prayed this prayer, trust that God has heard you, and take the next step to join a local church community.

Background Materials

MOSES

Early Life in Egypt

Moses was born into a Hebrew enslaved family, but because of God's supernatural intervention, he was adopted by Pharaoh's daughter (Acts 7:20; 7:23–32) and raised in an Egyptian royal household.

It was here that Moses was taught the Egyptian beliefs and culture that equipped him for a future role beyond his wildest imagination.

Exile in Midian

At forty, Moses went into exile and fled to Midian after committing murder. He would spend forty years in the wilderness tending sheep herds. In those years Moses got married to Zipporah, the daughter of Jethro, a Midianite priest.

Leadership of Israel

After spending decades in Midian, Moses, now much older, returned to Egypt, where God called him to lead the Israelites out of slavery. It was during their forty-year journey through the wilderness that God used Moses to reshape the people's identity. Through him, God gave the Israelites the law and guidelines for how they were to live as God's chosen people.

EZER

ʿēzer (translated as "helper") a Hebrew word that conveys strength and the ability to intercede. This word is used in some instances throughout Scripture in military contexts to describe someone who rescues, defends, and provides vital aid in times of crisis.

It reflects the very nature of God as our rescuer and defender. This is why *ēzer* is most often used in Scripture to describe God. In Psalm 46:1, God is called our *ēzer*, our "ever-present help in trouble."

ĒZER KENEGDO

This term is used in Genesis 2 to describe a helper that is equal to the man, one who corresponds to him but is opposite to him as a true counterpart.

GLORY

kavod (כָּבוֹד), a Hebrew word for "glory," communicates the weight and expression of God's character, His holiness, righteousness, and power.

doxa (δόξα), the Greek word for "glory" in the New Testament, refers to God's reputation and the revelation of His greatness, splendor, and worth, particularly in the person and work of Jesus Christ.

TWO TYPES OF COVENANTS IN THE ANCIENT NEAR EAST

In the ancient Near East, covenants were central to political, social, and spiritual relationships. More than legal agreements, they defined the bond between rulers and their people or between two parties. It was common for words of the covenant to be carved into stone or clay to signify their permanence and weight. They were usually sealed with oaths. (Example: Ex. 19:7–8.)

Suzerain-Vassal Covenant

This occurs when a powerful ruler (the suzerain) makes an agreement with a weaker entity (the vassal). The suzerain offers protection, resources, and military support in exchange for the vassal pledged loyalty and obedience.

Royal Grant Covenant

The suzerain (the stronger party) bestows valuable assets such as land or territory to a faithful servant.

(See 2 Sam. 7:12–16 and the Abrahamic covenant in Gen. 12:1–3; 17:1–8.)

TABERNACLE

In the New Testament, the Greek word for tabernacle is *skēnē* (σκηνή), which means "tent" or "dwelling." It comes from the verb *skēnóō* (σκηνόω), meaning "to dwell" or "to pitch a tent." One of the most explicit connections between the tabernacle (Ex. 13:21–22) and Jesus appears in John 1:14.

Just as God's glory filled the tabernacle, Jesus, the Word made flesh, "tabernacled" among us and took up residence not in a tent but in a human body.

CHURCH

Ekklesia, the Greek word for church that represents "an assembly" or "a gathering." It comes from the root *ekkaleo*, meaning "to call out." It's a community specifically called out for a purpose (1 Peter 2:9). Buildings didn't define the early church; people did. These imperfect people were filled with the Spirit (Acts 2:4), living as temples of God's presence, and seeking to reflect His glory in every corner of their lives.

PARABLE

Parable, *Parabolē* (παραβολή), is the Greek word meaning "to place alongside" or "to compare." It's what we use in English to describe two truths that run together side by side.

Parables are stories that illustrate one idea alongside another to clarify its meaning by comparison.

Jesus' use of parables was not simply to offer "an earthly story with a heavenly meaning," a phrase often attributed to the theologian William Barclay.

The comparative nature of Jesus' stories invites listeners to perceive how the kingdom of God reveals itself through Jesus and His kingdom mission.

MERITOCRACY

Meritocracy exists when people in a society or cultural group assess and treat individuals according to their abilities, achievements, or contributions to society.

IMPARTIALITY

God does not judge based on a person's visible status or lack thereof. God's sees beyond wealth, influence, or merit. God evaluates every human heart with perfect justice and righteousness.

IMPARTIAL LOVE

God's radical and generous hospitality to welcome undeserving sinners, regardless of their power, position, or past. God's impartial love does not leave sin unaddressed. It must be dealt with either through the work of Jesus on the cross or through eternal separation from Him. This balance of grace and justice is a core aspect of God's impartial love.

PARTIALITY

A sin that involves showing preferential treatment or bias toward specific individuals or groups based on shallow and superficial criteria rather than character or actions. Scripture condemns partiality because it distorts justice while it undermines equality.

BROKERAGE

A broker brings two parties together to make an agreement, functioning as an intermediary.

PATRONAGE

A system in which a rich and powerful person (the patron) helps someone with less power (the client) by offering support, protection, or resources. In return, the client gives loyalty and services.

GOLD RINGS

James 2:2 uses "gold rings," literally meaning "gold fingers." The interpretation relies on the cultural context for its understanding. In the first century, people wore gold rings to demonstrate their wealth, social status, and authority. The noble and elite flaunted them as outward signs of their influence.

In James 2:2, the gold rings serve as an example of how people tend to judge others based on external appearance.

Acknowledgments

First and foremost, I want to give all glory and thanks to God, for without His supernatural strength and sustaining power, this study would not be possible.

I want to recognize two remarkable scholars: Old Testament professor Dr. James E. Allman, who has given me the privilege to study under his wisdom for the last three years; and scholar Eugene McKinnon, whose conversations and guidance over this past year have helped me love the Bible more than I ever imagined possible. I am deeply grateful for you both.

Though no words feel quite sufficient, I want to thank the Moody team for believing in this study and the gifts that God has placed within me. I want to specifically thank my editors, Erin Davis and Whitney Pipkin. Your commitment and support have served this study well.

I want to give special honor to Colleen Nunn; your wisdom and dedication to prayer have transformed my walk with God over this last decade.

They say you're supposed to save the best for last, so I want to give a heartfelt thanks to my family, friends, and coworkers; you saw in me what I couldn't yet see in myself. Your hope and belief in God's work in my life breathed life into this study. Thank you!

NOTES

The Impartial Plan of God

1. The Bible Project, "The Shema: Listening to God," https://bibleproject.com/explore/the–shema/.

2. Howard F. Vos, *Nelson's New Illustrated Bible Manners and Customs: How People of the Bible Really Lived* (Thomas Nelson, 1999), 417.

Week One: Impartial Creator

1. Howard F. Vos, *Nelson's New Illustrated Bible Manners and Customs: How People of the Bible Really Lived* (Thomas Nelson, 1999), 55.

2. Warren Baker and Eugene Carpenter, *The Complete Word Study Dictionary: Old Testament* (AMG Publishers, 2003), 6754.

3. Baker and Carpenter, *The Complete Word Study Dictionary*, 6754.

4. John Walton and Craig S. Keener, eds., *NIV Cultural Backgrounds Study Bible* (Zondervan, 2016), 3.

5. Carol L. Meyers, *Discovering Eve: Ancient Israelite Women in Context* (Oxford University Press, 1988), 196–98.

6. Meyers, *Discovering Eve,* 72–94.

7. Sue Blundell, *Women in Ancient Greece* (Harvard University Press, 1995), 42–43, 68–70.

8. Blundell, *Women in Ancient Greece*, 42–43, 68–70.

9. Blundell, *Women in Ancient Greece*, 42–43, 68–70.

10. Jessica L. M. Jenkins, "Transforming Eve's Legacy in Genesis," We Who Thirst, https://wewhothirst.com/transforming–eves–legacy–in–genesis/.

11. Baker and Carpenter, *The Complete Word Study Dictionary*, H68.

12. Baker and Carpenter, *The Complete Word Study Dictionary*, H5828.

13. Bill T. Arnold, *1 & 2 Samuel*, NIV Application Commentary (Zondervan Academic, 2003), B. 4, 5.

14. Walton and Keener, *NIV Cultural Backgrounds Study Bible*, 12.

15. Walton and Keener, *NIV Cultural Backgrounds Study Bible*, 12.

16. John H. Walton, *The Lost World of Adam and Eve: Genesis 2–3 and the Human Origins Debate* (IVP Academic, 2015), 128–39.

17. Michaela Bauks, "Sacred Trees in the Garden of Eden and Their Ancient Near Eastern Precursors," chapter "Trees as Symbols of Fertility," *Journal of Ancient Judaism* 7, no. 3 (2016): 271.

18. The Bible Project, *Design Patterns in Biblical Narrative (Study Notes)* (The Bible Project, n.d.), 9–13.

19. The Bible Project, *Design Patterns*, 9–13.

20. Marcia Pally, *Commonwealth and Covenant: Economics, Politics, and Theologies of Relationality* (Eerdmans, 2016), 17

21. Walton and Keener, *NIV Cultural Backgrounds Study Bible*, 224–25.

22. Sharon H. Ringe, "Jesus and the Jubilee: Probing Images of Liberation," in *Jesus, Liberation, and the Biblical Jubilee: Images for Ethics and Christology* (Fortress Press, 1985), 14, 50, 91.

Week Two: Impartial Covenant

1. John H. Walton, *Ancient Near Eastern Thought and the Old Testament* (Baker Academic, 2018), 71.

2. John Walton and Craig S. Keener, eds., *NIV Cultural Backgrounds Study Bible* (Zondervan, 2016), 33.

3. John H. Walton, *The NIV Application Commentary: Genesis* (Zondervan, 2001), Toledot of Noah (6:9–9:29): Covenant (9:1–17).

4. Robert Alter, *The Hebrew Bible: A Translation with Commentary* (W. W. Norton & Company, 2018), 347, Kindle Edition.

5. E. Randolph Richards and Richard James, *Misreading Scripture with Individualist Eyes: Patronage, Honor, and Shame in the Biblical World* (IVP Academic, 2020), 4.

6. Guy Prentiss Waters, J. Nicholas Reid, and John R. Muether, eds., *Covenant Theology* (Crossway, 2020), 138.

7. Waters, Reid, and Muether, *Covenant Theology*, 139.

8. Hebrews 6:13.

9. Michael Horton, *Introducing Covenant Theology* (Baker Publishing Group, 2009), 31.

10. Walton and Keener, *NIV Cultural Backgrounds Study Bible*, 23.

11. Walton and Keener, *NIV Cultural Backgrounds Study Bible*, 23.

12. Howard F. Vos, *Nelson's New Illustrated Bible Manners and Customs: How People of the Bible Really Lived* (Thomas Nelson, 1999), 16–17.

13. F. F. Bruce, *The Book of the Acts*, New International Commentary on the New Testament (Eerdmans, 1988), 50–53.

14. The Holy Bible, New International Version® (NIV®), NIV Study Bible. Copyright 1995 by The Zondervan Corporation. All rights reserved. Page 43.

15. Walton and Keener, *NIV Cultural Backgrounds Study Bible*, 62.

16. Waters, Reid, and Muether, *Covenant Theology*, 261.

17. Referencing the stories in Matthew 26:26–28, Luke 22:19–20, and John 6:53–56.

Week Three: Impartial Communion

1. John Walton and Craig S. Keener, eds., *NIV Cultural Backgrounds Study Bible* (Zondervan, 2016), 23, 255.

2. Warren Baker and Eugene Carpenter, *The Complete Word Study Dictionary: Old Testament* (AMG Publishing, 2003), H8641.

3. Clothing is used both to represent God's righteousness (Isa. 61:10; Zech. 3:3–5; Matt. 22:11–14; Eph. 6:14) and the effects of sin and unrighteousness (Gen. 3:7–10; Zech. 3:3–4; Isa. 64:6).

4. Walton and Keener, *NIV Cultural Backgrounds Study Bible*, 11.

5. The Bible Project, "Were Adam and Eve Priests in Eden?," https://bibleproject.com/articles/were–adam–and–eve–priests–eden/.

Week Four: Impartial Call

1. John Walton and Randy McCracken, "Revolutionary Revelation in a Cultural Package," *Bible Study with Randy*, July 2020, https://www.biblestudywithrandy.com/2020/07/revolutionary–revelation–in–a–cultural–package/.

2. John Walton, *Ancient Near Eastern Thought and the Old Testament 2nd ed.* (Baker Academic, 2018), 88–91.

3. Walton, *Ancient Near Eastern Thought and the Old Testament*, 94, 95.

4. Willem A. VanGemeren, *Interpreting the Prophetic Word: An Introduction to the Prophetic Literature of the Old Testament* (Zondervan, 1996), 38, 385–389.

5. Katie M. Heffelfinger, "Isaiah 40–55," in *The Oxford Handbook of Isaiah*, ed. Lena–Sofia Tiemeyer (Oxford University Press, 2020), 111–13.

Week Five: Impartial Christ

1. Howard F. Vos, *Nelson's New Illustrated Bible Manners & Customs: How the People of the Bible Really Lived Thomas Nelson, 1999*, 380, "Agricultural Workers," "Merchants."

2. Howard F. Vos, *Bible Manners and Customs: How People of the Bible Really Lived* (Thomas Nelson, 1999), 417.

3. Janice P. De–Whyte, *Wom(b)an: A Cultural–Narrative Reading of the Hebrew Bible Barrenness Narratives*, Biblical Interpretation Series, vol. 162 (Brill, 2018).

4. Janice P. De–Whyte, "(In)Fertility in the Ancient Near East," in *Wom(b)an: A Cultural–Narrative Reading of the Hebrew Bible Barrenness Narratives* (Brill, 2018), 24–52.

5. George T. Montague, *Mary's Role in the Incarnation through the Lens of Luke* (2024), 7–9.

6. John Walton and Craig S. Keener, *NIV Cultural Backgrounds Study Bible* (Zondervan, 2016),

7. Walton and Keener, *NIV Cultural Backgrounds Study Bible*, 1608.

8. Eusebius of Caesarea, *Ecclesiastical History,* trans. and annot. Paul L. Maier (Grand

Rapids, MI: Kregel Academic, 2007), 37, PDF excerpt, accessed June 11, 2025, https://www.kregel.com/books/pdfs/excerpts/9780825433078.pdf.

9. Fredrick Dale Bruner, *The Christbook: A Historical/Theological Commentary*, vol. 1 (Word Books, 1987), 6.

10. Frederick Dale Bruner, *Matthew: A Commentary. Volume 1: The Christbook, Matthew 1–12* (Eerdmans, 2007), 7.

11. Mishnah Rosh Hashanah 2:2, https://www.sefaria.org/Mishnah_Rosh_Hashanah.1.8. "Legal and Religious Status of Jewish Females," *Jewish Women's Archive*, https://jwa .org/encyclopedia/article/legal–religious–status–of–jewish–female.

12. Warren Baker and Eugene Bruner, *The Complete Word Study Dictionary: Old Testament* (AMG Publishers, 2023), G4637.

13. A. M. Hunter, *Interpreting the Parables* (SCM Press Ltd, 1960), 8.

14. Brad H. Young, *The Parables: Jewish Tradition and Christian Interpretation* (Hendrickson Publishers, 1998), 3.

15. Hunter, *Interpreting the Parables*, 150.

16. Young, *The Parables: Jewish Tradition and Christian Interpretation*, 3.

17. Young, *The Parables*, 3.

18. *Mishnah Sotah* 3:4, Sefaria, https://www.sefaria.org/Mishnah_Sotah.3.4.

19. Walton and Keener, *NIV Cultural Backgrounds Study Bible*, 1779.

20. *Menachot 43b, The William Davidson Talmud*, trans. Koren-Steinsaltz, https://www .sefaria.org/Menachot.43b.17.

21. *Menachot 43b, The William Davidson Talmud*.

22. Lynne Hilton Wilson, "Jesus' Atonement Foretold Through His Birth," in *To Save the Lost*, ed. Richard Neitzel Holzapfel and Kent P. Jackson (Brigham Young University, 2009), 103–26.

Week Six: Impartial Church

1. Randolph Richards and Richard James, *Misreading Scripture with Individualist Eyes: Patronage, Honor, and Shame in the Biblical World* (IVP Academic, 2020), 82–85.

2. Richards and James, *Misreading Scripture with Individualist Eyes*, 82, 83.

3. James C. Scott, *The Moral Economy of the Peasant* (Yale University Press, 1976), 27.

4. John Walton and Craig S. Keener, *NIV Cultural Backgrounds Study Bible* (Zondervan, 2016), 2164–65.

5. Walton and Keener, *NIV Cultural Backgrounds Study Bible*, 2164–65.

6. Warren Baker and Eugene Carpenter, *The Complete Word Study Dictionary: Old Testament* (AMG Publishers, 2023), H5375 נשׂא (nāśā'), H6440 פָּנִים (pānīm).

7. Douglas J. Moo, *The Letter of James* (Eerdmans, 2021), 91–93.

8. *The NIV Study Bible* (Zondervan, 1985), 1879.

9. Walton and Keener, *The NIV Cultural Backgrounds Study Bible*, 2164–65.

10. E. Randolph Richards and Brandon J. O'Brien, *Misreading Scripture with Western Eyes: Removing Cultural Blinders to Better Understand the Bible* (InterVarsity Press, 2012), 110.

11. Walton and Keener, *The NIV Cultural Backgrounds Study Bible*, 196, on verses 16:1–2.

12. *NIV Study Bible* (Zondervan, 1995), 1445, on Matthew 5:5.

13. Baker and Carpenter, *The Complete WordStudy* Dictionary, H3519 כָּבוֹד (kābôd).

14. "Footstool," *Encyclopedia of the Bible*, https://www.biblegateway.com/resources/encyclopedia–of–the–bible/Footstool.

15. *NIV Study Bible*, Fully Revised Edition (Zondervan, 2020) 1644, 16:18.

16. *NIV Study Bible*, Fully Revised Edition 1463, 16:18.

About the Author

Oghosa Iyamu, daughter of Nigerian-born parents, is a Bible teacher and theologian passionate about sharing the truth of God's Word in a way that brings freedom. With over twelve years of experience in full-time ministry, she studied at Dallas Theological Seminary and later earned her Master of Divinity (MDiv) degree from Southwestern Baptist Theological Seminary. Oghosa has written "Verse of the Day" stories for the popular Bible app YouVersion, and contributed to platforms such as She Reads Truth, Lifeway, Radical (a ministry by David Platt), Lies Young Women Believe, (In)Courage, and more. She currently resides in Atlanta, GA, where she is a freelance writer. To learn more, visit OghosaIyamu.com or follow her on Instagram @OghosaIIyamu.

This Bible study is part of a growing line of rich, deep Bible studies from Moody Publishers.

MOODY PUBLISHERS
WOMEN
BIBLE STUDIES

IN-DEPTH.
CHRIST-CENTERED.
REAL IMPACT.

If God Is For Us
A 6-week Bible study on Romans 8
by Trillia Newbell

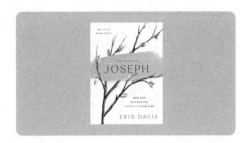

The Story of Joseph
An 8-week Bible study of through the genealogy of Joseph
by Erin Davis

7 Feasts
An 8-week Bible study in the sacred celebrations of the Old Testament
by Erin Davis

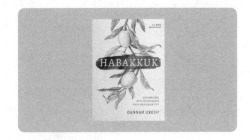

Habakkuk
A 6-week Bible study on Habakkuk
by Dannah Gresh

The Way Home
A 6-week Bible study of Ruth
by Tessa Afshar

Before the Throne
An 8-week Bible study on prayer during difficult times
by Crickett Keeth

Explore more Bible studies to dwell & delight in God's Word at
MOODYPUBLISHERSWOMEN.COM